ISBN 978-1-332-21621-5
PIBN 10299517

1 MONTH OF
FREE
READING

at
www.ForgottenBooks.com

By purchasing this book you are eligible for one month membership to ForgottenBooks.com, giving you unlimited access to our entire collection of over 1,000,000 titles via our web site and mobile apps.

To claim your free month visit: www.forgottenbooks.com/free299517

English
Français
Deutsche
Italiano
Español
Português

www.forgottenbooks.com

Mythology Photography **Fiction**
Fishing Christianity **Art** Cooking
Essays Buddhism Freemasonry
Medicine **Biology** Music **Ancient**
Egypt Evolution Carpentry Physics
Dance Geology **Mathematics** Fitness
Shakespeare **Folklore** Yoga Marketing
Confidence Immortality Biographies
Poetry **Psychology** Witchcraft
Electronics Chemistry History **Law**
Accounting **Philosophy** Anthropology
Alchemy Drama Quantum Mechanics
Atheism Sexual Health **Ancient History**
Entrepreneurship Languages Sport
Paleontology Needlework Islam
Metaphysics Investment Archaeology
Parenting Statistics Criminology
Motivational

Infants in Institutions

A Comparison of Their Development with Family-Reared Infants During the First Year of Life

---

SALLY PROVENCE, M.D.

ROSE C. LIPTON, M.D.

Yale University Child Study Center

Preface by

MILTON J. E. SENN, M.D.

INTERNATIONAL UNIVERSITIES PRESS, INC. • NEW YORK

PART I
BACKGROUND AND METHODOLOGY

PART II
THE INSTITUTIONAL ENVIRONMENT AND
THE INFANT'S EXPERIENCE

PART IV

FOLLOW-UP AND IMPLICATIONS

APPENDICES

vii

Preface

ONE OF THE MOST definitive concepts of child development specifies that prolonged deprivation of maternal care affects adversely the personality development of children. Many studies in Britain and the United States during the past fifty years have produced evidence of various kinds to demonstrate the particular harm that may come to infants who are institutionalized, or whose care in other settings has similarly been defective in mothering, especially when this has been distinguished by discontinuity, insufficiency, or distortion. Bowlby's monograph on maternal care and mental health published by the World Health Organization in 1951 was not only an exhaustive review of world literature and a summary of his own studies, but included theories about the influence of maternal deprivation on the child's personality. Bowlby's indictment of nurseries and other institutions, particularly hospitals, had a widespread and dramatic influence on improving the care of children in institutions. Moreover, his work has stimulated in the past ten years much research aimed at clarifying the issues and providing new evidence in support of Bowlby's thesis or in contradiction of it.

The research reported here by Provence and Lipton does more than support the evidence that children in institutions are affected adversely under certain conditions of inadequate mothering when compared to children reared in families where a mother was continuously present and provided care which was sufficiently nurturing to foster optimum development. Going beyond an identification of maldevelopment induced by poor maternal nurturance, this report is a detailed analysis of the results of such deprivation, with special focus on the processes in human development vulnerable to damage. This study not only compares two groups of babies in the first year of life and in a sense is cross-sectional; it has the greater advantage of being longitudinal as well. Short-term in extent, it examines babies over a period of ensuing time and is an example of antrospective longitudinal research which aims to determine how the mother-child interaction affects the processes of child development and hence of personality formation. The study differs too from most on this subject by assessing the influence of maternal care on a variety of facets of the personality. Furthermore, whereas other authors preferred to measure results broadly in terms of changes in intelligence quotients or developmental quotients, or of shift in traits of character such as in friendliness and willingness to speak, Provence and Lipton analyzed the infant's behavioral responses in detail. For example, speech formation was not reported as size of vocabulary or as gross speech impediment, but rather as to the nature of the sequences of its development and the types of vocalization used in communication. Similarly, other symptoms of deprivation such as defects in socialization, thought conceptualization, and the impairment in capacity for making close affectual ties were appraised minutely in the variegated forms in which they appeared.

This research is what has been characterized as a "stuff of life experiment," or, as the authors prefer to call it, action research. Being aware of the difficulties of the experimental method, the prototype of laboratory research, the authors set about to collect data systematically through clinical observation and structured testing. Their work is a fine example of clinical research based on observations by experts. Studies made previously had demonstrated that not all damage from maternal deprivation is sufficiently gross to be obvious at a crude level of observation, and this negative finding led to some doubt as to the severity of such influence. This study, using more refined methods of observation and paying minute attention to detail, carefully documents the scope of deprivation. Combining astute clinical experience and objective assessment with structured, standardized tests enabled the authors to obtain valuable, rich, and fascinating data which they interpret in a highly imaginative way.

This research is noteworthy then not only because of the carefulness of the studies made, but because of the relevance and pertinence the findings have for care of babies unfortunate enough to be separated from their mothers. Research which disavows any responsibility except that of being objective may well qualify as "pure," but it is a kind of purity which today is often overvalued in our society. In the life of deprived children there are things that need not so much to be considered philosophically as things that need to be acted upon. It seems to me that the authors in this monograph marshaled their facts and presented them lucidly, and with a conviction that they had a responsibility to improve the lot of children by influencing what people do to them.

MILTON J. E. SENN, M.D.

Introduction

This report is based upon a research study of institutionalized infants in which their development was compared with that of infants living in a family setting. We report here the findings of the first year of life. It is written mainly for professional people who are concerned directly with the care of infants and who are in a position to help promote their development.

The family—father, mother, and children—is the setting in which babies can best be provided with the care and influences that support and foster good development. It becomes increasingly hard to provide such care as we get farther away from this model. The infant's needs are multiple and complex, and it is difficult or perhaps impossible to meet them adequately under conditions of group care.

This report will attempt to be specific about why we believe this. It is not a polemic against any institution or its staff. It is a plea for better care of babies, for we believe with others that the first year is of great importance in the life of the individual.

We hope that the presentation and description of some of the specific aspects of infant development will enable those who work with or in behalf of children to look at them and their environment more closely and to try to understand some of the things that are involved in the intricate and complex process of development.

Acknowledgments

We should like to express our thanks to the Field Foundation, New York, and to its executive director, Maxwell Hahn, for encouragement and financial support of this research project. We are pleased to acknowledge the considerable contributions of Milton Senn who originated the research, of Katherine Wolf who was a valued consultant in its planning phase, and of Ernst Kris whose enthusiasm for the data was a source of great stimulation. Through the several years of data collecting and writing our colleagues have discussed the material or read the manuscript with interest and care and for their help we are particularly grateful: Laura Codling, John Doris, Dorothy Inglis, Marianne Kris, Edgar Lipton, Seymour Lustman, Audrey Naylor, Richard Newman, Eveline Omwake, Samuel Ritvo, Albert Solnit, and Mary Stark. Lottie M. Newman has not only contributed her skill as an editor but has made valuable suggestions as to content. Demetra Parthenios, Arlene Richter, Sophie Dutton, and Paul Hartmann have recorded, typed and duplicated countless pages of data and manuscript. Finally, we express our appreciation for the collaboration of the staff of the institution in which these data were collected and for the cooperation of the social workers in the child-placement agencies responsible for the foster-home care of the children.

PART I

Background and Methodology

Background and Methodology

IN THE THIRTEENTH century Frederick II, German King, King of Sicily and Emperor of the Holy Roman Empire, directed an experiment which yielded unlooked-for results. It is described in a quotation from Salimbene to which Stone and Church (1957) have called attention:

> ... he wanted to find out what kind of speech and what manner of speech children would have when they grew up if they spoke to no one beforehand. So he bade foster mothers and nurses to suckle the children, to bathe and wash them, but in no way to prattle with them or to speak to them, for he wanted to learn whether they would speak the Hebrew language, which was the oldest, or Greek, or Latin, or Arabic, or perhaps the language of their parents, of whom they had been born. But he laboured in vain, because the children all died. For they could not live without the petting and joyful faces and loving words of their foster mothers. And so the songs are called "swaddling songs," which a woman sings while she is rocking the cradle, to put the child to sleep, and without them a child sleeps badly and has no rest.

This bit of data from 700 years ago suggesting the importance of maternal care has gained supporters in more modern times.

Bowlby (1951) has made a comprehensive review of the world literature in which he summarized and commented upon many of the reports, designating the classes of evidence and types of studies undertaken. He makes the point that

[3]

many observers, working in different settings with varying methods, have demonstrated the adverse influence of maternal deprivation upon the development of young children.

The evidence that Bowlby presents gives great weight to the belief that institutional living, with the lack of adequate maternal care that characterizes this experience, has a damaging effect upon the development of infants and young children. The damage has usually been described as progressive deterioration, and little attention has been given to the variety of symptoms by which the syndrome of "hospitalism" can manifest itself. Consequently, the comparison of institutionalized children with family children has chiefly been made in terms of "better" or "worse" using primarily developmental or intelligence quotients obtained from tests rather than in terms of specific differences or similarities.

One of the needs for research into the influence of deprivation has been for studies in which the specific deficit in the care of the child can be described and the effect evaluated. Although efforts have been made to delineate this in one area or another, e.g., to evaluate the influence of certain types of child care, the data usually available are incomplete. In many studies that have been reported it appears that a recognizable deficit in maternal care is often an expression of a more general attitude of the mother which influences not only the area on which the investigation focused but other areas of the child's development as well. The lack of awareness of the multiple factors involved has resulted in an oversimplification of the problem. It has led to generalizations about the effects of maternal deprivation based upon incomplete data and seems to have contributed to some of the current confusion and contradictions in the literature. We believe that only detailed phenomenology of children in institutions, based on both physical and psychological studies such as this research has

[4]

utilized, can eliminate the confusion between the syndrome of "hospitalism" or "affect deprivation" and other conditions such as congenital handicaps, constitutional variations, or consequences of physical illness.

It was under the impact of the data and ideas expressed in the preceding paragraphs that this research study was initiated. The report is concerned with a description and evaluation of a group of institutionalized infants in the first year of life, with the environment in which they lived, and the comparison of these infants with infants reared in a family setting.

In designing our study and planning the methodology we were concerned with the following points.

1. We attempted to describe the institutional environment in detail in order to understand what was present and what was absent in the infants' experience.
2. We measured, rated, and described in various ways the behavior, development, and reactions of the infants over a period of time.
3. We tried to establish that the infants were free from congenital handicaps, neurological disorders, and acute or chronic illness.

We present in the following paragraphs the general aspects and major points of the methodology to orient the reader and to facilitate the communication of our findings.

The 75 institutionalized infants whom we studied were all drawn from the population of one institution in which we worked over a five-year period. All examinations of the babies, observations of the environment, and interviewing of staff were done by the two investigators.

The environment for the group was observed in respect to its physical characteristics, the size of the staff, the atmosphere created by the staff members and their attitudes, child-care practices and policies. The environment of the individual infant was also observed as it has long been recognized that the experiences of individual babies may differ rather widely within the same setting.

The sequence for each visit was as follows: one of the observers went into the nursery to get the baby and asked a few questions about his immediate state (health, relation to feeding, etc.). He was brought to the examining room where the test was administered by one of us, while the second simultaneously dictated observations independently to the secretary. Each observer scored the test items and any differences were reconciled by referring to the detailed recording or by repeating the item. The infant was then given the pediatric and neurological examinations by the second observer, and measurements of length, head, and chest circumference were made.

The infant was then returned to his nursery and the attendant was interviewed on the spot. Summaries of the testing, observations, and interview material were made within twenty-four hours after the visit. The records of each examining session consisted of five types of data:

1. Infant Tests—the Gesell Developmental Examination and the Hetzer-Wolf Baby Test from the Viennese Scale.
2. Physical and neurological examinations.
3. Measurements of height, weight, head and chest circumference.
4. Observations of behavior and reactions not included in the tests. We considered this an important part of our data because it was essential to be as specific as possible about how the similarities and differences between babies manifest themselves.

5. The persons who care for the baby were interviewed in regard to their observations of his developmental progress, health, and various aspects of his care and his behavior.

Family history, birth and previous history were obtained in so far as they were known.[1] Incidental observations of the babies were made at times when we were there primarily to examine another baby. These informal contacts provided some additional data on each infant.

One of the things that had to be established for all babies, in so far as present clinical methods permit, was the freedom from congenital handicaps (mental and physical), neurological disorders, and acute or chronic disease. Some of these disorders, especially in the first year of life, are accompanied by symptoms that may be difficult to distinguish from those produced by maternal deprivation. This is one of the reasons for the longitudinal method and for repeated observations. In some of the institutionalized infants, the freedom from congenital mental subnormality could be established with certainty only after they had left the institution and were living in a family environment.[2]

[1] This refers to the well-known fact that it is often very difficult to obtain accurate information about the family background of institutionalized babies.

[2] While this is described as part of the methodology it is also one of the findings of the study: when an infant in an institution shows signs of retarded development, one cannot clarify the question of his basic endowment as long as he remains in a situation of deprivation. One of the aids to diagnosis in clinical medicine in general is that of response to the therapeutic trial. This procedure employs that principle: if the infant's improvement is adequate after the introduction of more adequate nurturing, one can exclude gross central-nervous-system damage or defects and gross congenital mental subnormality. One cannot exclude very mild degrees of equipmental impairment, however, because the residual effects of severe deprivation in infancy and the residual effects of minimal cerebral damage or dysfunction are similar in many ways. This is a point which requires further research into the relationships between psychic and somatic processes in the earliest years of life.

[7]

In an attempt to control some of the variables that would complicate the evaluation of the data we set up several additional criteria: we chose to include in the study only those babies who were admitted to the institution under three weeks of age; we excluded from the study group any infant with an obvious handicap of any kind; also excluded was any baby who was prematurely born and any who had a recent severe illness or operation. Some of the excluded infants were the subjects of separate studies; they are referred to later in Chapter 17 on Differences in Vulnerability, but they are not included in the main groups of babies.

Some infants were examined every four to six weeks throughout the first year. These are the babies upon whom we have the most data. In order to increase the study population and to test the observations made on the more intensively studied infants, we examined others at longer intervals. For these, there were three to five examining sessions at various selected ages during the first year. In addition, all study babies who left the institution were examined one or more times after they had been placed in a family environment.

Since the findings in regard to the less frequently examined infants are the same at comparable ages as those examined more often, we report them together.

The 75 babies reared in families with whom the institutional babies are compared have been seen by the same investigators in two other research projects and in a clinical service for the developmental evaluation of children at the Child Study Center of Yale University. This comparison group of family-reared infants was subjected to the same criteria for selection, and studied with the same methods as the institutional group.

2

Point of View

EVERY RESEARCH study reflects the orientation and point of
view of the investigators. Since there are many approaches to
the study of child development and many attitudes toward the
data derived from observation, we set forth our approach in
order to make our findings clear.

The two investigators came to the study from a background
in pediatrics followed by training in child development which
included techniques of infant observation and testing. To this
had been added an opportunity to participate in a longitudinal
study of child development originated by Milton J. E. Senn
and Ernst Kris at the Yale University Child Study Center.
This research project studied children who were living in their
own families and while the data were more extensive than
those obtained in the institutional study, it utilized many of
the same methods of evaluation of the infants. For several
years the studies went on concurrently, providing an opportunity to compare the two groups of babies.

The combining of physical and neurological data obtained
through pediatric examinations with the data of infant testing
and observation and the consideration of psychological factors
in the evaluation of development are basic to the study and to
the way in which the data are presented.

Since so much of the material is based upon the infant tests
we wish to indicate the way in which we have used them.

[9]

The Use of the Infant Tests for Measurement
and Observation

The particular infant tests used in this study were the Gesell Developmental Examination and the Hetzer-Wolf Baby Test from the Viennese Scale. Since they became popular in the 1930s the baby tests variously called psychological tests, intelligence tests, and developmental examinations have been widely used in clinical work and in research. After receiving an initially enthusiastic reception, the tests have fallen into disrepute among many professional ·people. In particular, there has been disappointment that the test scores during the first year of life are not more reliable predictors of intellectual functioning at a later age. For a time the tests were misused, especially in adoption work, through a misunderstanding of their assets and limitations. Emphasis was placed on the test score and utilizing this score, professional people attempted to "match" infants and adoptive parents, e.g., an infant who earned a high test score would be placed in a family with high intellectual standards. This attitude stemmed from an unwarranted belief in the fixed nature of "endowment" and a narrow concept of the developmental process. It also reflected the understandable wish to be more precise in assessments of human characteristics and the propensity for worshiping a score as unimpeachably scientific. Bayley (1940, 1949) has written of the limited value of the scores on infant tests for prediction of later I.Q. scores. Escalona (1950) has pointed out, however, that there are other and more valuable uses of the infant tests; e.g., they contribute behavioral data which can be utilized for predictive purposes (see also Escalona and Moriarty, 1961).

In our experience, the infant tests have proved to have considerable diagnostic and predictive value, when one considers not mainly the score, but other characteristics of the infant that are revealed by the test. This does require an understanding of the complexities of development and of the various factors that can influence it.

Thus we believe that the infant test when carefully used can be a procedure of considerable value, and that like all observational methods it has assets and limitations and is reliable only in the hands of people trained to use it.

The 1959 report of Escalona and Heider describing their Infancy Project and the follow-up study indicates how the infant tests can be used as one of the methods of observation. Their report contains, in our opinion, the most thoughtful and comprehensive discussion currently available of some of the complex problems of research in infancy; in addition, it presents a careful and helpful conceptual view of developmental processes.

In what follows we shall summarize some of the characteristics of the infant tests as well as our evaluation of their usefulness.

The data from the test situation can be characterized as derived from (1) the quantitative assessment and (2) the use of the test as a structured observation situation.

1. *Quantitative Assessment*

This designates what the infant does compared with the normative standards upon which the tests are based. This quantification requires the presentation of the test situations or tasks in the standardized way and the recording of the infant's success or failure on the individual items. Such a procedure establishes the developmental age or general maturity level in weeks or months on the test scales. From this a developmental quotient can be computed, which is a comparison of the infant's developmental age with his chronological age. The developmental age or quotient is an indicator of the infant's level of functioning at that particular time. It inevitably reflects the influence of multiple forces and is the product of the interaction between the infants innate endowment and the influences of the environment. When the inborn apparatuses are intact and the environment is favorable one will see a test performance that produces an average or above-average test score. If there is damage, defect, or delayed maturation of the apparatus or if the environment is grossly inadequate, one will derive a score below the norm. This low score, in itself, however, does not reveal the cause of the developmental delay. Moreover, it does not necessarily imply an unfavorable outcome, since it may be based upon factors that can be influenced by therapeutic intervention.[1]

The quantifiable data from the tests can also be organized so that the levels of functioning on the various test items can be compared with each other. In respect to the significance of such comparisons, Escalona and Leitch (1953) have suggested that "marked discrepancies between maturity of behavior in different areas of development (as assessed by infant tests) reflect developmental deviations and are associated with disturbances in the adequacy of the child's adaptation to the social, biological and physical environment. Irregular levels of maturity displayed within a single test area may also reflect a disequilibrium in the child's adaptation to the demands of everyday existence."

The developmental profile is a graphic method of compar-

---

[1] For example, the development of infants suffering from metabolic disorders such as congenital hypothyroidism is vastly improved by administration of adequate doses of thyroid hormone. Similarly, an improved environment can bring about improvement in the test scores of infants whose delayed development is due to deficits in the environment. The use of test scores for prediction of later development must take into account a wide variety of conditions that can interfere with development.

[12]

ing developmental age or maturity levels in the various sectors measured by the test. One can show on a graph, for example, the relationship of the score in the motor area with language, or perception with social development. Spitz (1945, 1946) and Spitz and Wolf (1946a) made use of this method of presenting data in their reports on hospitalism in infants. This is an interesting device and has some merit, but it also has some serious limitations, particularly if one tries to use it to suggest the etiology of a developmental disorder. These limitations are imposed partly by the weaknesses of the tests, but mostly by the complexity of human development itself. It is difficult —or more correctly, impossible—to divide behavior and development into neat categories which are of the same order and the same meaning at all ages. If one looks, for instance, at a sector such as social development on the tests, one sees that not all items are comparable. Some are very direct indicators of the infant's awareness of and responsiveness to people, while others are much more related to styles or preferences in child care. For example, the infant's extending a toy to a person for the purpose of initiating a social interchange is an observation of different relevance from that of whether he drinks from a cup. Both are items standardized on the Gesell scale at the same age. Both undoubtedly reflect some aspect of his experience with people, but they are not of equal significance. Similarly on the Hetzer-Wolf test the item in the social area at month VI measures the infant's capacity to imitate the facial expressions of the examiner; at month XI-XII it assesses his response to the presentation of a new activity (the manipulation of two hollow blocks). A failure on the social item at six months cannot be assumed to have the same diagnostic significance as a failure on the social item at twelve months. One therefore must avoid the error of placing too much reliance upon the profiles for diagnostic purposes. While they do have

[13]

some value, they give the illusion of a degree of scientific precision that is not borne out on close examination.

We believe that much can be learned by a careful scrutiny and comparison of the individual items passed and failed at the various age levels. We have found this method of evaluation of the data very rewarding in a research study of infants in their own families and in the clinical diagnostic service at the Yale University Child Study Center as well as in the research we are reporting here. For example, in the institutionalized infants we encountered a remarkable consistency in respect to the individual items passed and failed on the tests. There proved to be certain constellations of findings that were characteristic of the babies reared in this environment. While there were individual differences in the degree of retardation, the specific deficits were uniform and fell into definite patterns.

Other constellations can be found in other situations. There are some items on the test that are of particular value in the assessment of the neurological status of the infant. In fact, the use of the developmental tests as a functional neurological examination has, in our experience, contributed important information in the differential diagnosis of developmental problems.

2. The Use of the Test and the Test Situation As a Structured Observational Setup

This is a method that has nothing to do with the quantitative scores on the tests. It consists of two major areas: (1) *how* the infant does what he does with respect to the test items, and (2) his other reactions and modes of behavior that become easier to describe because they occur in a structured context familiar to the observer. This gives the observer an additional helpful methodological tool. It is easier to organize the data

[14]

of observation—and indeed to observe more carefully and with fewer omissions—when one has seen many babies in a similar situation. This applies not only to the study of human behavior but to a variety of other situations as well, and is one of the reasons for systematization in any area of observation.

Among these observations made in the course of the test, the areas selected for attention naturally reflect the interest of the observer and the focus of the diagnostic or research study.

One can observe output and tempo of movement, organization of movement patterns, promptness of response to a stimulus, impressions of energy and modulation of discharge of impulse. Comparisons can be made between activity characteristics and reactivity to stimuli.

One can describe the attention span and the capacity for concentration or the degree of distractibility. This can include an assessment of the extent to which the child is aware of other stimuli without being disorganized by them. An assessment can be made of his disorganization of function (or resistance to it) under the impact of fatigue, hunger, absence of the mother, coincidental illness, or other stressful situations. Responses to transitions from one test situation to the next may arouse discomfort or anxiety in some infants. The degree of anxiety produced at any point and how the infant reacts to it can be judged, as well as his modes of dealing with it and with other types of discomfort. One can estimate such things as the degree of attention and investment in the self, in the adult, in activities, and in the test materials, or the infant's reactions to and interactions with the examiner and the mother.

The varieties of behavior which reflect the repertoire, spectrum, and intensity of feelings can be observed as well as the infant's individual mode of expression.

There are other characteristics of behavior that can be observed, but the above should be sufficient to make the point.

[15]

It is important that the observations be systematic and that the behavior observed be recorded. The interpretations and inferences drawn from the observations will reflect the experience and orientation of the investigators.

One of the most interesting uses of the tests and the observations that can be made in the course of them concerns their usefulness for the understanding of personality development. Psychoanalysis as a developmental psychology implicitly and explicitly acknowledges the importance of biological forces. In addition to the importance of the innate instinctual drives, it recognizes the importance of the inborn apparatuses in the development of the personality. Hartmann (1939) speaks of the importance of the somatic and mental apparatuses as they influence the development and functions of the ego which uses them; he speaks of these apparatuses as one of the roots of the ego. He indicates that such functions as perception, motility, intelligence, memory, and others rest upon constitutional givens and he designates them as components of the ego constitution. The inborn apparatuses are brought successively into play through the maturational process which is largely intrinsic, though it is influenced by environmental factors.

Hartmann poses an important question in a form that provides a stimulating approach to research in infant development. He says, "We reject the customary form of this question: what is biological and what is psychological in the developmental process? We ask instead: what part of it is congenital, what maturational, and what environmentally determined? What physiological and what psychological changes take place in it?"

Kris (1951b) has suggested that tests and measurements may make their main contribution to the study of child development through their value for the assessment of the autonomous ego functions. While this is an important point, we believe

[16]

that in the behavior that can be observed around the tests one can also gain important clues about the nature of a child's relationship to people, his areas of conflict, and some of the defensive maneuvers he is likely to employ.

In evaluating the test observations, therefore, we suggest that they can be viewed in the light of some of the many questions implied in Hartmann's formulation. A careful assessment of a baby's development can yield information about various aspects of his status: it tells something about the growth and maturation of his inborn neurological and physiological equipment; it says something about the extent to which he is able to make use of his equipment in his adaptation to his environment; it gives some clues to the nature and adequacy of his personal relationships, especially the relationship to his mother. One can observe in an infant's behavior various aspects of the differentiation and mode of functioning of the mental apparatus. For example, one can find evidence of a gradually increasing awareness of reality; there is the developing appreciation of the self as different from another person; there is the growing distinction between persons and inanimate objects, and there are signs of remembering; there is a gradually increasing capacity to act in a purposive way, to communicate, to solve problems, to seek pleasure, to avoid unpleasure, and to express loving or angry feelings toward others. Some of these ways of behaving appear to reflect quite directly the processes and influences that play a part in them. In others, as will be seen in the material, the connections are inferred.

A brief example will illustrate a few of these points: when a baby of eleven or twelve months creeps across the room to find and play with a ball that he has seen disappear under the sofa one observes the influence of many interacting forces. Such an act requires coordination of trunk, arms, legs, hands, and eyes; it indicates that he perceives and has developed some

[17]

interest in a toy, can be attentive to it, remembers it for a time when it is out of sight, and can make use of it; it reveals his capacity to act in a voluntary way to obtain something that attracts him. Such behavior implies many of the things that are mentioned in the paragraphs above. If his inborn equipment is damaged or defective, he will not be able to go and find the ball. Additionally, the data of this study show that he also will not be able to act in this way if he has been deprived of the variety of experiences involved in good maternal care.

GENERAL THEORETICAL ORIENTATION

We view infant development as a dynamic, unfolding process based upon a complex set of interactions between the baby, with his unique characteristics, and his environment. In his environment we include, as being of paramount importance, the attitudes, feelings, and actions of his mother in all of the ways in which she provides care for him and relates to him.

One of our major interests has been to look at the similarities and differences between the institutionalized babies and babies who have had more adequate mothering in the hope that the comparison would help us to understand some of the processes and interactions through which development and learning take place in the first year of life.

The deprivation suffered by infants in institutions is believed to be related to several factors:

1. *The absence of a specific maternal figure* with all that this implies. One refers here to the need of infants to be cared for mainly by one person in order to promote adequate mental and emotional development. The multiplicity of individuals that share in caring for institutionalized infants results in a fragmentation of care and lack of constancy that are believed

to make it more difficult for an infant to develop an awareness of himself and his environment. It appears to exert a retarding influence on learning in a general sense.

2. *The shortness of time* spent in the care of the infants. This is a quantitative deficit. Though it is not possible to delineate exactly what amount of care is optimal for the development of a particular infant, and the margin of safety is probably rather wide, there is no doubt that there is a need for a certain quantity of maternal care below which the infant's development definitely suffers. Most infants living in institutions do not get enough mothering in purely quantitative terms.

3. *The lack of personalized care* refers to two things. First, the interest and emotional involvement of the person who cares for the baby in an institution can only in the very rarest instances be compared to a mother's attachment to her own baby. The relationship between mother and baby contains both positive and negative feelings. In the innumerable interactions between mother and baby day after day, her interest and feelings are communicated in various ways. These communications, which provide one of the most important elements in the infant's development, are reduced to a minimum in institutionalized infants. The second important lack of personalized care is that the care given in most institutions is of necessity routinized and is only occasionally related to the needs of a particular infant at a given moment. For example, he is fed, diapered, lifted up, and put to sleep on a schedule that is almost exclusively externally determined. The infant thus has very few experiences in having the adult respond to his needs (e.g., the discomfort of hunger) at the time he expresses them, and thus his opportunities to learn what (and

[19]

later who) it is that brings comfort or pleasure are very meager.

These three points, in condensed and summary form, anticipate much of what will be said in this report.

NOTES ON TERMINOLOGY AND ORGANIZATION OF DATA

The child development literature is extensive and terminology varies depending upon the training and orientation of the writer.

For the sake of clarity we have tried to be consistent in the use of certain terms which might otherwise be ambiguous. We have used the word *maturation* not in its broadest general sense but to refer specifically to the process of growth and differentiation of the infant's inborn apparatus. We use the term *apparatus* to include body structures, physiological processes, and intrinsic possibilities for growth and differentiation with which the human infant is born. We have referred to the way in which the characteristics of the infant are expressed, i.e., his way of being, as *function, development,* or *behavior.*

The term *stimulation* is used in at least two different ways which should be clear in the context of the description. It is used to indicate an appeal to the various sensory modalities: tactile, kinesthetic, visual, olfactory, acoustic, etc., either singly or in combination. It is also used to describe aspects of the contact with another person; e.g., social and emotional stimulation involve communication of various feelings through the sensory modalities and this implies considerably more than a simple stimulus-response system.

One term which will be encountered frequently in this report is the word *investment.* In using this, we intend to convey something about the infant's interest in or attention to another person, a toy, or an activity. It implies that he is able to direct toward the outside world some kind of energy, attention, or interest in an active way.

[20]

It is apparent, since we used infant tests in our study, that we might have focused in this report on the comparative test scores of the two groups, utilizing statistical correlations. Since our data, interpreted statistically, do not reveal new findings, we have chosen not to emphasize this aspect, although some relevant material is contained in the Appendices. In this respect, our material confirms the work of those who have reported a progressive decline in scores on infant tests as a result of severe deprivation of maternal care.

Perhaps the most interesting and significant findings from the infant tests in the babies are related to the surprising consistency of the institutionalized babies in respect to individual test items passed or failed. This finding, which forced itself upon our attention, required that we look carefully at the constellations of success and failure. We found that the specific deficits were remarkably uniform and followed a similar pattern in all infants. It was this set of findings in particular which has led us to examine the nature of the environment and mode of child care for some of the explanations of the development and characteristics of the institutionalized babies. These findings are tabulated in Appendix B.

In what follows the material is organized under various headings. Part II contains a description of the environment and its deficits. Part III deals with the development of the infants during the first year of life. Our findings are presented in these categories: Motor Behavior; Reactions to People, Feelings and Emotional Expressiveness; Language; Reactions to the Inanimate Object; Discovery of the Body and the Sense of Self. There is a chapter that discusses some aspects of individual differences in vulnerability to the conditions of the institutional environment. In the final chapter of this section the development of an institutionalized and of a family infant are compared. Material dealing with perception, activity, passivity, oral behavior, and autoerotic activity is included in the various sections. The divisions are arbitrary and there is overlapping, but some device was necessary in order to organize the material and facilitate its presentation. Part IV presents follow-up data and deals with some of the practical applications of the findings.

PART II

The Institutional Environment

and

The Infant's Experience

3

The Institutional Environment

THE INSTITUTIONALIZED infants lived in a three-story building like a conventional school building with large, open rooms
opening off long, wide hallways. The building, while not of
recent construction, was kept in excellent repair and always
appeared scrupulously clean.

As one entered the institution and walked along the halls to
reach the rooms where the infants lived the atmosphere was
one of order and cleanliness with a lingering aroma of food
odors, cleaning solutions, etc., that might be characterized as
an "institutional" smell. An unusual degree of quietness was
an outstanding feature. It seemed incredible that 75 children,[1]
from the ages of four days to six years were living here. Occasionally, one encountered in the halls a group of fifteen to
twenty-five two- to three-year-old children accompanied by one
or possibly two attendants as the group moved to the dining
room, playroom, bathroom, or sleeping room. The groups appeared unusually quiet and orderly in comparison to a similar
age group of nursery school children, for example. The quietness and orderliness of these groups disappeared as soon as the
children saw the investigators;[2] a large part of the group would
cluster around us, with uplifted arms, and the children who

[1] Average census.
[2] The children were in no way familiar with the investigators as the study
involved younger children and such encounters in the halls did not occur with
any frequency or regularity.

[25]

had been most recently admitted to the institution would call, "Mommy," a cry often taken up by others.

The infants studied were housed in two separate nurseries in which the basic equipment of cribs and clothing was simple but adequate. However, playpens, supportive chairs for young infants, and high chairs were few in number. This situation seemed to result from the staff's unawareness of the contribution such equipment might make to children's development.

The younger group of infants (age four days to eight months) occupied cribs placed singly in glass-partitioned cubicles. The room was clean, cheerful, and light, with adequate heat and ventilation. A radio, softly played, often gave forth popular music. The infants were fed in their cribs with bottles propped. When cereals, pureed fruits, and vegetables were added to the diet, they were also given in a propped bottle with a large-holed nipple rather than given by spoon. Bathing, dressing, and diapering were done on a table in the central work area. The infants under four months of age were rarely out of their cribs except for bathing, dressing, and diapering, although occasionally the supportive chair was used for a baby who was thought to be "advanced" or for a baby whose crying seemed excessive to the staff. Sometimes a stuffed toy was placed in the crib for the baby to look at. After about four months of age simple rattles, beads, etc., were placed on a string suspended across the crib sides and the single playpen, which contained other age-appropriate toys. The playpen was used in an unplanned way depending on the attendant's ideas and her reaction to the various individual babies' behavior toward the toys and the infant who might be sharing the playpen with him. For example, a baby who regularly threw toys out of the playpen or "attacked" another baby was much less apt to be placed in the playpen than a baby whose behavior was more acceptable to the attendant.

Each infant in this group shared the time and attention of the attendant with seven to nine other infants in the same age range for the eight-hour period of the day when she was present. For the remaining sixteen hours of the day there was no person in the nursery except at feeding time when an attendant who also had similar duties in other nurseries heated formulas, propped bottles, and changed diapers. Her presence could lead to no more than the briefest of contacts because she had twenty-five to thirty other babies for whom she must do the same before it was time to start over again. The most consistent person in each baby's life was the attendant who was with him during an eight-hour day, five days a week. During those hours his contact with her was mainly in being taken from his crib to the work area once daily for bathing and dressing, and subsequently three or four times for a diaper change.

The older group of infants (age nine to twenty-four months) lived in a large, uncubicled room with many windows. The room was located in another area of the same floor and did not connect with the other nursery except via the central hallway. The cribs were arranged side by side in pairs in two long rows, which were separated from each other and from the walls by wide passage ways. Space was adequate for twenty babies and at times there was overcrowding as the census temporarily increased. The room was light, cheerful, with adequate temperature control and ventilation.

A sink cabinet was centrally located along one wall, and at bathtime two cribs near the sink were used for sponge bathing and dressing. Dressing and diapering at other times were done in the baby's own crib, the nurse taking the necessary equip-ment with her from the central storage cabinet.

This older group of about twenty infants was cared for by two attendants during the day, with a third person assisting at feeding times. They were fed three meals a day with milk by cup also after the midday nap. Most babies no longer sucked from a bottle. While the staff professed to an attitude of encouraging self-feeding, only two high chairs were available for the group so that there was no regular opportunity for an individual baby to have self-feeding experiences. Each infant was fed in his own crib lying on his back with a diaper placed under his chin. After about age eighteen months he was fed sitting up in a corner of his crib.

After breakfast each child was bathed and dressed in a competent, rapid, and rather mechanical fashion. If he could walk fairly steadily, he was placed on the floor, given a toy, and allowed to move freely about the nursery. Those babies not yet walking were either returned to their cribs or placed in the one playpen in the nursery, two or three at a time and given a few toys. This play period usually lasted for one to two hours and was repeated in the afternoon after their naps. During these "play" periods the attendants were occupied with housekeeping duties and usually interacted with children only when a child cried, generally from being unable to get or to do something he wanted. Some crying resulted from one child taking another child's toy, but since there were duplicates available and since the children had only desultory interest in toys, there were comparatively few conflicts. There was some play between children which they initiated and seemed to enjoy; such play occurred between children in the playpen or between two children in adjoining cribs and consisted of looking, touching, smiling, and exchanging toys, or bouncing, rocking, and running up and down in imitation of the other child.

Diapering was done in the individual child's crib after lunch, naptime, supper, and again before going to sleep for the night. It was a routinized procedure and usually not adapted to a baby's activity of the moment.

The children had no experiences outside the walls of the nursery except on rare occasions when a child might be taken out for some medical procedure or the testing done as a part of this study.

While there were two regular attendants for the older group during an eight-hour period, five days per week, infants were not regularly assigned to the same attendant. This meant that these infants had even less in the way of a consistent personal relationship than the younger group had. For the remaining sixteen hours of the twenty-four-hour period the group was left unattended, except for the person who had duties in other nurseries as well. She diapered them and put on their pajama pants, the final step in preparing them for sleep.

The staff in both nurseries seemed to like the babies and gave as much of themselves as they could under the conditions imposed by the policies and practices of the institution and by their own personalities. The educational background of the administrative staff as well as the personnel giving direct care to infants was limited, and no one in either group had had any specific training in the developmental needs of infants and young children. The administrative staff qualified for their roles on the basis of having knowledge of institutional management and the education of school-age children. Other staff members were selected on the basis of their being women who "liked" children.

Some staff members were observed to be especially interested in and responsive to an individual baby. Such a special relationship was more apt to occur between the younger infants and their attendants than in the older group. Some nurses spoke of their reluctance to have such a relationship because they had once or twice had a "favorite" and their own separation experience had been sufficiently painful so that they did not wish to repeat the experience. Other attendants said they had never had a "favorite" and spoke with pride about liking all the babies the same.

From the outset the staff showed little interest in the study, the investigators, or the study findings, except to ask how an individual baby had performed on the developmental test and to want a statement concerning his performance for their records. They occasionally asked for medical consultation regarding a baby's condition or asked about a child who they knew was being followed after he left the institution. They otherwise asked nothing of the research staff. Offers made to participate in staff conferences and training (both were nonexistent) were accepted as an idea, but were never acted upon. The resistance to changes in child-care practices was also noted when other groups and individuals tried to stimulate interest in initiating changes within the institution. The staff was always patient and tolerant, extending themselves without complaint for the project, which at times must have been burdensome even if it only meant answering the telephone a few more times in a given day. They provided the facility for the study but were never a part of it in a cooperative way, nor was there any possibility of the institution's utilizing the knowledge gained from the project to bring about changes that altered the care of the children.

4

The Feeding Experience

We select the feeding experience of the institutionalized group for detailed description, not only because of the importance and repetitious nature of feeding, but because it represents a major difference in the lives of the institutionally reared infants as compared to the family-reared infants. By contrasting the experience of the two groups greater understanding of the complicated process known as "maternal care" and its influence on infant development is anticipated.

The institution carefully provided a diet for all infants that was nutritionally appropriate for physical growth. However, the staff was never large enough to provide anything more than a propped bottle[1] for the infants under eight months of age. Thus, from the earliest weeks of life the institutionalized infant did not come to associate his state of discomfort arising out of hunger and the comfort derived from being fed with a human being, nor did he receive the wide variety of sensations associated with being held by his mother.

Feedings for the youngest infants (0 to 4 months) were given every four hours, six times daily, except for an occasional infant who was considered small by weight and was fed every three hours. Feeding times were fixed according to the institution's routine, and there was little chance for modification to meet an individual infant's needs. If a baby was crying when the attendant began to prepare the group, he might receive his

---

[1] Occasional and rare exceptions.

bottle first; if he was asleep, he was awakened to eat. Prior to feedings each infant was diapered and returned to his crib where he was placed on his side with a blanket roll at the back to prevent rolling. The nipple was placed in his mouth and the bottle propped on a small pillow. The attendant worked quickly in order that the other seven to nine infants could be fed.

It should be remembered that while a baby is prepared to suck at birth, his ability to keep a firm, continuous grasp on the nipple is not good and only develops slowly over a period of several months. Moreover, the ability actively to reach out with his hands, find the displaced bottle, and replace the nipple in the mouth occurs only after seven to eight months of age. The youngest institutionalized infants lost the nipple frequently, and its return and their continued sucking were entirely dependent on the attendant. If she was watchful and not otherwise occupied or if the baby cried loudly enough to get her attention, the nipple might be returned promptly. More often the nipple was returned after some delay. If an infant cried and seemed hungry in advance of the regular feeding time, his chances of being fed promptly were poor because of the attendant's manifold duties and because of the sixteen-hour period of each twenty-four hours in which the attendant was present in the nursery only intermittently and at long intervals.

During feeding the institutionalized infant experienced virtually no change in the quality or quantity of outside stimulation except for the presence of the nipple in the mouth. As he was fed in his crib, he received some stimulation from the surface of his crib where his body touched it, from his own body where it was in contact with another body part, from his clothing, and what he could see and hear around him. However, he was stimulated to a similar degree and by the same sensations most of the rest of his waking hours as he lay in his crib.

The infant who is held for feedings by his mother has an enormously different experience and set of sensations. As he is picked up and held his body position is changed radically from lying on his back or abdomen; he no longer is stimulated only by the crib mattress and other parts of his own body but rather by the contact with her body and the varying pressures she places on his buttocks, back, etc.; he makes many postural adaptations as he is picked up, carried, and then placed in a feeding position. In contact with her body he experiences changes in temperature; as he is carried about he sees, hears, and smells; he experiences a human contact, a social interchange with all the variety of both positive and negative emotions. The experience of being fed in an emotionally enriched environment is a point of major difference from the institutional procedure.

In addition, the baby in a family has experienced these sensations that bring comfort and satisfaction to him much, or perhaps most, of the time in response to his distress signals. Thus, he gradually learns to make some connections between his expression of discomfort and the response of the other person. This opportunity for learning is not part of the experience of the institutionalized babies as they are fed on an externally determined schedule which has little to do with their individual state of comfort or discomfort.

As the institutionalized group approached four to five months the diet was supplemented by cereals, pureed fruits, and vegetables. However, the new foods were added to the formula and were given by bottle using a nipple with enlarged holes. The babies missed the opportunity of being fed in the upright position with new implements, e.g., a spoon. The experience did not provide them with much change in tastes and textures; they continued to use the nipple only, lying in the crib with the bottle propped. As these babies grew older they were better able to retrieve the nipple if they lost it than they had been earlier. It might be expected that since no one held their bottles they would be able to do so at an early age, but this was not the case, and in comparison to the family-reared group they were older when they held their own bottles. Their inactivity during feeding was striking.

At varying times during the six- to nine-month period all the institutionalized babies recognized the bottle, discriminating between it and a doll of the same size (an item from the Hetzer-Wolf test). This occurred at a time when they did not discriminate between the attendant and the examiner. This is a reversal of the sequence of events seen in the family-reared infant in whom the signs of discrimination between people appear earlier than signs of discrimination between inanimate objects.

It has been established, through observation of infants cared for by their mothers, that if they have had a good feeding experience, one sees the beginning development of a capacity to wait briefly for the feeding by the time they are four to five months of age. Such a developing capacity can be observed when a baby who is crying to be fed stops his crying and watches as his mother prepares the feeding. This behavior is believed to indicate several things: he perceives what his mother is doing, and this perception evokes the memory of previous feedings, i.e., of experiences in which his hunger discomfort has been relieved by the ministrations of the feeding person. This interaction of perception and memory produces an anticipation of the future, i.e., that he is about to be fed, and thus he is able to wait a little while for his feeding. The capacity to wait begins mainly around satisfactory feeding ex-

[34]

periences and naturally is also influenced by other experiences of the infant in which some kind of discomfort, tension, or distress is relieved by the nurturing person. Benedek (1938) first referred to this phenomenon as the baby's developing a feeling of confidence in the mother. Erikson (1950a) refers to it as the sense of trust.

It is noteworthy that the institutionalized babies showed no signs of developing a capacity to wait for feeding based upon the sense of confidence or trust in the adult. When the bottles, or later the food, appeared and they were able to recognize it, some cried and appeared eager. Although they had waited many times before out of necessity, they had developed no true capacity for waiting; they behaved as if they did not know whether they would be fed and could only believe it when the bottle reached the mouth. Others were docile and quiet but gave no indication that they looked forward to a pleasurable experience. Some appeared overwhelmed by their need and unable to wait; others seemed depressed. One might speculate whether these latter had learned that crying was of no use, but of this we cannot be sure. What one can be sure of is that there was no evidence of the capacity to wait with anticipation in any of the institutionalized babies in the first year.

The encouragement to be active about some of the feeding other than the bottle (e.g., to feed oneself a cookie or cracker) was not offered. The ever richer and more complex communications that pass between mother and baby around feeding during this age period were virtually absent. The infant's experience instead of being more varied and enriched remained narrowly constricted, although maturationally he was ready for a larger world and a more complicated interchange with his environment.

In the second nursery (age nine to twenty-four months) the picture was similar. The twenty babies in this nursery were cared for by two attendants during the day. A third person assisted at feeding times.

Three meals a day were given and additional milk following a midday nap period. Most babies took milk from a cup and no longer sucked from a bottle, the weaning process having been carried out in the nine- to twelve-month age period with a gradual substitution of the bottle by cup. At mealtimes the practice was to feed each infant in his crib lying on his back. After about age 18 months he was usually allowed to sit up in a corner of his crib for meals.

The attendant averaged about six to eight minutes feeding each baby. The meal characteristically consisted of a bowl of either cooked cereal or soup to which other foods, such as meat, vegetables, or fruits, were added. A dessert such as ice cream was given separately. The bowl of semisolid food mixture was held close to the infant's face and quickly and efficiently spooned into his mouth. While the infant was not actively restrained, any attempts he made to move about for whatever reason were discouraged by the attendant's words, tone of voice, and facial expression.

The children were almost unbelievably inactive during this process, only rarely attempting to touch the spoon, bowl, or attendant, although they watched her face attentively. The attendant was usually pleasant in her ministrations in the few minutes while she prepared a baby for feeding and removed his bib afterward, but the interchange during the entire period was minimal. The staff seemed to believe that such social interchange would prolong the time required to feed by exciting the babies and making them "uncooperative." They more often talked to each other than to the babies they were feeding.

The children who were known to take the longest to feed, for whatever reason, were usually fed last, although they often gave signs of being the most eager to eat when the meal cart appeared in the nursery.[2] Some attendants took the attitude "he must learn to wait his turn," while others said as many children as possible should be fed while the food was warm.

Letting the children do some self-feeding, except for their being given a piece of bread or cookie occasionally, was a rare occurrence. Two high chairs were available for the group of about twenty, and there were no regular opportunities to have self-feeding experiences with the help of an adult.

Thus, the feeding experience for a baby in this age group continued to be a deprivation of massive proportions. In fact, the feeding practices at this age actively interfered with his use of motor patterns he could use to feed himself and fostered the passive lying on the back of the suckling age. While the nipple was supplanted by the spoon and a semisolid food mixture replaced the formula, it was no more a social experience with a person interested in helping the baby use his developing skills and capacities than it had been earlier.

The importance of the feeding experience to the growth, health, and psychological development of infants has received considerable attention from many writers. Ribble (1943) discusses the opportunity that breast feeding affords for communication between mother and infant and for the fondling and handling that seem to be necessary for growth. Brody (1956), in a comprehensive presentation of feeding practices which included an extensive review of the literature, makes the point that feeding is also the first important experience in mutual adaptation between mother and infant. The baby is not merely a passive recipient in this situation; some participation is required from him if the feeding is to be satisfactory. The fact that this participation on his part in the earliest days

2 Dr. Marianne Kris, in hearing this observation, has speculated that the babies who kept their eagerness may have done so because, since they were difficult to feed, they necessarily received more attention during feeding.

occurs as far as we know without conscious awareness does not detract from its importance as an adaptation which will gradually and almost imperceptibly merge with something that can later be recognized as learning. Of at least equal importance is the beneficial influence on the mother of the success of the early feeding. Erikson (1950b) speaks of the importance of mutual regulation of behavior of mother and baby to the success of the feeding. Greenacre (1960) says that "the infant begins by having to work for a living at nursing and continues by taking over gradually and with the mother's cooperation the other concerns of his body life."

At birth the infant is endowed with reflexes which orient him to feeding and permit him to ingest the food. If the area about the lips and cheeks is touched lightly, a reaction occurs in which the head and tongue are moved toward the stimulus. The infant rotates his head to one side; the tongue moves toward the stimulus, and sucking movements of the mouth occur even when the stimulus remains inaccessible. The reaction, which occurs more quickly than it can be described, is more pronounced when the infant is awake and hungry. Spitz (1955a) notes the already complex interrelationships of the early feeding experience as the hungry infant is picked up to be fed. He points to the links between the feelings in the mouth and those of hands, skin and inner sensations, and makes the crucial point that all of these sensations are inseparable from the feeling of comfort that ensues as feeding proceeds.

The feeding experience for the human infant, bringing him stimulation through the channels he has for receiving them, e.g., sight, hearing, taste, smell, touch, and position sense, provides much more than the intake of sufficient food nutrients and calories for his bodily growth and maintenance. He receives a wide range of communications expressed by the

[38]

mother through her emotional responses to him and through her body as she talks to him, carries, holds, cuddles, and shifts his body about for their mutual comfort.

It can also be viewed as the experience around which he first begins to organize and be aware of some of the sensations and perceptions that accompany the mother's ministrations. Out of his hunger and physiologic need for feeding he feels discomfort. His expression of this discomfort brings his mother who holds, feeds, and makes him comfortable again. This total sequence—the contrasting states of tension due to discomfort which is followed by relief when his need is met—is believed to be of great importance in many aspects of an infant's growth, development, and learning. As he grows a little older and with the many repetitions of being fed, he slowly learns to recognize and to form an attachment to the person who feeds him. Anna Freud (1954) suggests that in the earliest months his attachment is to the experience of satisfaction and relief brought about by the ministrations of the mother and not so much to her as a specific person. However, this early stage is the first step toward the development of a personal relationship and the baby's attachment shifts gradually from the experience of satisfaction to the person without whom the satisfaction would not have come about. With this step forward, the infant begins to develop a loving relationship with another person which grows gradually and becomes more complex as time passes.

One can summarize our main points about the feeding experience as follows:

Feeding is a biologically and psychologically crucial experience in the first year around which there are many communications between mother and baby. There are feelings which may be loving, tender, exciting, anxious, hostile, or varying mixtures of these. Without discussing what feelings or combinations of feelings are helpful or potentially harmful, the point we wish to make is that feelings seem to be transmitted and that these contribute to the child's development and to his learning about the world. Many sensory experiences are involved in it as well.

It is difficult to overestimate the importance of the feeding experience as an organizing and integrating force in the life of the infant. Around it he takes his first steps in the development of a relationship to others. The multitude of stimuli that are inherent in it and the activities that are a part of it provide him with a wealth of learning opportunities without which satisfactory development is difficult or impossible.

The deprivation of the institutionalized infant in this experience was one of many dimensions: he received little stimulation; there was a lack of opportunity to adapt and be adapted to; the sight, sound, feel, smell of another person who did something that made him comfortable or gratified were rarely experienced; the important step in learning that one can make another person appear as a result of calling, crying, or giving some other signal did not occur.

All these and many other experiences that surround the normal feeding are things of which the institutionalized babies had only the faintest glimmer. Their caloric intake was adequate, but they missed many things of great importance to their development.

There are other important daily experiences in the life of a baby which are considered in the following chapters.

5

The Bath

THE BATH was the activity around which there was the longest personal contact with the attendant and the greatest amount of stimulation. The babies were sponge-bathed on the worktable with soap and water; the skin was usually oiled or powdered. If the baby had any skin rash, this was a time for applying medication.

The nurse usually talked to or smiled at the baby as she quickly and efficiently went through the bathing process and the dressing that followed. She might also tweak his toes, tickle his belly, or pat his back. Her emotional relationship with each baby varied according to her own personality and the appeal he had for her.

After he was dressed he might be held up and talked to face to face for a moment, after which he was carried back to his crib. This bath period, which for most babies comprised fifteen or twenty minutes, encompassed his most concentrated and consistent experience with another person, and it was during this time that one saw his greatest activity and social responsiveness. One could imagine it as the high point of the day for him. It was a combination of skin and muscle stimulation, sights, sounds, and social contact.

His bath differed from that of a family baby in various ways. It was undoubtedly more efficiently and quickly accomplished by the attendant than most mothers could do it, but more important than the time or skillfulness involved was the fact that even in the earliest months, there are many more communications of feelings from a mother to her baby than occurred with the institutionalized babies. Some of a mother's feelings are loving, tender, and protective; some are anxious—especially with the first baths; occasionally there is anger. The point is that the mother's interest and emotional involvement are transmitted in this situation as in all the others. In addition, especially in the second six months, there are many experiences for a family baby that are a part of his learning more about and enlarging his world, e.g., becoming accustomed to the feeling of being in the water and what one can do or cannot do with it; grabbing for toys or powder can; squeezing a sponge, sucking the washcloth, trying to eat the soap, poking into the mouth of the faucet or trying to catch a drop of water; being warned away from the hot water tap, being allowed to splash a little but not too much; having his excitement both permitted and controlled. The bath is usually a pleasurable and stimulating time though it can also be unpleasant—or it may be a mixture of pleasure and unpleasure. Here, as in other situations, the sensory and perceptual experiences are mingled with a variety of emotional states and exchanges with a familiar and important person.

The institutionalized babies had no such variety or rich experience. The deficit existed for them partly because of the routine and unvarying procedure and partly because of their low investment in people and in the environment that became increasingly apparent as a part of their developmental problem as the first year proceeded.

6

Diapering

Dıapers, which were used two together without waterproof pants, were changed four to six times daily for most of the babies. The baby was taken from his crib to the worktable; the skin was sponged with water and oiled or powdered. The shirt and outer clothing were also changed if they had become wet or soiled. The entire process was brief but provided a personal interchange and some sensory stimulation. The time of changing was determined by the routine of the nursery and not when the baby might express discomfort. The diapering seemed to be one of the punctuating events of the day, and with it the babies had some mothering which they enjoyed, but its relationship to their own state of comfort or discomfort was inconsistent.

While there is a wide range of maternal behavior in regard to all aspects of diapering, i.e., frequency of changing and emotional responses to the infant, the family infant is more apt to be diapered in response to his signals of discomfort than is the institutionalized infant. Diapering may represent for the institutionalized infant much more of a peak experience than it does for a family baby. For the former it is one of the few times in his day when he is held, moved to a place other than his crib, and experiences a social contact.

7

Sleeping Behavior

WE DO NOT have detailed information about the sleeping behavior of the babies in the institution. Reports obtained from the staff suggest that the infants slept longer hours and with fewer interruptions than babies in families. The children were prepared for naps and for bed at night at regular and designated times. The rooms were darkened and activity within the nurseries ceased as staff members were off duty or worked elsewhere at these times. If a baby consistently cried a great deal,[1] he became known to the staff and was given an extra feeding or placed in a supportive chair. In the absence of crying, babies were assumed to sleep well. It may be that they did sleep more than family babies as there was so little in the experience to make it attractive to stay awake, but we have insufficient data to support or refute this assumption.

The reports of foster mothers in regard to the sleep behavior of infants coming from this institutional setting into the family indicate that wakefulness and interruptions of sleep are extremely rare. More often one hears that for several weeks, the sleep was considered excessive and that a reduction in total hours of sleep accompanied the general improvement in the infant's development in response to an improvement in nurturing care.

[1] Babies who cried persistently were extremely rare. In a five-year period the institution never had a baby with "colic."

[44]

8

Interaction with Others

THE POSSIBILITIES for contact with another person were sharply limited in the experience of the institutionalized babies. Those contacts that occurred around the feeding, bathing, and diaper changing have been described. There were a few other possibilities. The attendant might pass a baby's crib on her way elsewhere and speak, smile, or stop to change his position. The attendant who brought the bottles of formula or the food cart from the kitchen might have a word for him. If a baby had a cold or some other illness, he was examined by the pediatrician and had his temperature taken by the nurse. If he needed medication, he received it. The staff was quite meticulous in caring for the physical health of the babies.

After he was five or six months old and could exert increasing control over his own position in the crib he could move in various ways to keep an adult in sight. From six months on the promptness with which anyone who came in the door of the nursery was looked at by the babies never failed to impress us. One could not avoid a feeling that a hunger for the personal contact was conveyed in this intense looking. If one did not speak or go to the baby, he would look elsewhere after a while and start to rock or finger some toy or part of his crib.

At times two of the babies of four to eight months would be put in the playpen together. They seemed, at this age, only mildly interested, however, and paid little attention to each other.

[45]

The babies in the nursery for the older group (nine to twenty-four months) were somewhat more interested in each other. The cribs were placed side by side in pairs in the large room of twenty to twenty-four children so that each baby's crib was against that of one other baby. Occasionally one would see a baby toward the end of the first year smiling at or touching his neighbor, but even with such proximity there was remarkably little interchange. Sometimes an older child nearing two years would toddle up to the crib of a younger one and look, rattle the crib side, or try to hand him a toy.

One of the deficits in the personal contact that seems of special importance in the institution group was that they were talked to so little. Speech is a crucial part of the interaction in which feelings and information are transmitted from mother to baby. There are many times in the life of the family baby when someone talks to him and reacts to his babbling. The family baby hears about how he feels, and what he is doing, about mommy or daddy or brother or the family pet; about the fact that he is sweet or noisy or wonderful, or that his face is dirty and he stinks; about a noise that frightens him or another that makes him smile; about what happens when he bumps his head or why he cannot pull his mother's hair. These and many more such statements, questions, exclamations, reprimands, and loving words are woven into the fabric of his everyday life. Though he only very gradually learns specifically what some of the words mean, they contribute in very important ways to his learning about himself, about others, and about the world. For the institutionalized babies such opportunities were meager. Nobody had time to talk to them enough about what went on in their lives. Nobody responded often enough with verbalized pleasure or feeling to the baby's vocalizations. Both from the standpoint of information and the communication of feelings that indicate that some things are more important than others, the babies experienced too little verbal contact. The impact that this deficit had upon their language development, emotional growth, and learning is elaborated in Chapter 14 entitled Language, and in Chapter 13 on Reactions to People, Feelings, and Emotional Expressiveness.

We believe that the poverty and the infrequency of the personal contact were the outstanding deficits in the experience of the institutionalized babies. It was a quantitative deficit in that there were not enough interchanges to promote development. It was also a qualitative deficit. While the attendants were pleasant to the babies and worked uncomplainingly and conscientiously, there was no relationship between nurse and infant that contained the variety and intensity of feelings a mother has for her own baby. The atmosphere as it appeared to the observer was mainly one of quiet, tranquillity, and blandness.

9

Experiences with Motor Activity

THERE WERE few situations in which the institutionalized babies were encouraged to be active motorically. They spent most of their time during the first year in their cribs. They were occasionally propped up in a sitting position in their crib or a supportive chair. During the bath they might be handled a little in such a way as to stimulate greater activity of legs or arms. When they were fed the premium was on being still and quiet, and they were fed mostly in the recumbent position throughout the first year; active participation in the feeding was not encouraged. Once they could get up on hands or knees or pull to stand, some adult might have a bit of time during the day to encourage them to creep or to cruise. If they showed signs of readiness for walking (this was usually only in the second year), they had a brief turn on the floor with support from the adult.

Most of their motor activity, however, was within the boundaries of the crib. It should be kept in mind that at most a child spent a total of four hours in a twenty-four-hour period out of his crib, and for a walking child this represents an enormous restriction of opportunities for motor activities. The stimulus and motivation to be active, that would come from being able to go after something attractive across the room or to move to get to the adult with whom one has fun or from whom one gets comfort, operated only to a very small extent here.

There were few opportunities and little motivation to be physically active.

[48]

10

Experiences with Toys

S UFFICIENT bright and attractive playthings appropriate to the age of the babies were a part of the environment. Some kind of toy was suspended over or placed in the crib of each baby. What one observed, however, was that there was very little playful activity on the part of the babies with the toys. We have attempted to explain the reasons for this lack of interest in play in the Chapter 15 on Reactions to the Inanimate Object.

What the babies missed was not the presence of the toy itself, but something that makes a toy interesting and worth while. The way in which this investment is related to the emotional tie to the mothering person is also discussed in Chapter 15 referred to above.

11

Sensory Stimulation

W E HAVE mentioned previously the meagerness of the institutionalized baby's experience in being touched, handled, cuddled, lifted, and talked to. His intake of visual stimuli was perhaps more adequate than others because he could look about largely independent of the presence or absence of the adult. He could see the attendant or his own hands or a blanket or toy, his crib, another baby, or the ceiling. He could bring about some changes in the scene by turning his head, rolling over, or sitting up. However, as he grew older in this first year, the visual environment, too, was much less rich and varied than that of the family baby. He did not see an automobile, an animal, a house, or a daddy. He did not have the experience of being taken out in the yard, for a drive in the car, or a walk in the carriage or stroller. He lived in his nursery and was taken out only very rarely and then usually to the medical room to be examined or treated. When he shifted from the first nursery to the second at nine months of age there were more children and a bit more activity. New toys appeared occasionally, and once in a while new people. On the whole, however, the environment remained much the same from day to day and month to month.

The monotony of what he could hear was perhaps even greater. The adults walked, talked, and carried out their duties with a minimum of noise. The other infants, too, made very few sounds, and one was perpetually surprised at the quietness of the nurseries. There was virtually no cooing or vocalizing, and even very little crying. The baby heard some adult talking and an occasional laugh independent of the contact someone had with him. He at times heard the sound of running water, the clink of nursing bottles, the closing of a door, a bell in the distance, or the sound of feet as the older children went past his nursery to the playroom. He might hear another baby cry or squeal or chuckle. He heard little else.

In summary, all forms of sensory stimuli that come to a baby from the outside were less than for the family baby—sights, sounds, touches, smells, whether singly or in combination with others were much less common in his life.

It is probable that with the sensory stimuli, as well as in other areas, the deficit was much more than a quantitative one. For the various sensations produced in any baby by outside stimuli have to be perceived, organized, and integrated with other experiences. While some of this integration no doubt comes from inner sources, an important part of it seems to be supplied by the mother through the experiences implicit in her care.

PART III

Description of Development During the First Year

12

Motor Behavior

Now that we have described the environment in which the infants lived, we turn to the descriptions of their development and behavior. We start with motor development because it is the area most easily described: it is readily accessible to direct observations, a fact to which the selection of test items attests. Moreover, it is through the motor system that many other aspects of development become observable.

On the infant tests motor behavior is assessed through a series of observations which include (1) locomotion and postural control in the supine, prone, and upright positions. This is generally referred to as gross motor development and reflects the status and control mainly of the larger muscles; (2) grasping (prehension) and manipulation which reflect skill in the use of the smaller muscles, especially those of the hands, and are referred to as fine motor development; (3) the co-ordination of various gross and fine motor skills.

In addition, we have systematically observed output of motor activity, muscle tonus, tempo and types of movements, and modulation of movement. We have also taken note, wherever we could identify them, of the various feeling states and emotions accompanying or expressed by the motor acts.

In the first three to four weeks of life the motor behavior of the institutionalized infants was not different in any way that could be measured from that of infants cared for by their mothers. There might have been seen some subtle differences in output of activity, for example, or predominance of various movement patterns if the infants had been observed more constantly, but no differences were noted with our methods of observation.

The first easily observable difference occurred in the second month and concerned a specific characteristic in the way the infants reacted to being held. There was a decrease in the extent to which they made appropriate postural adjustments to being held or carried. They did not adapt their bodies well to the arms of the adult, they were not cuddly, and one noted a lack in pliability. We do not refer to hypertonicity or muscle spasticity. All reflex behavior was normal. The best description is that they felt something like sawdust dolls; they moved, they bent easily at the proper joints, but they felt stiff or wooden as they were perceived through the holder's own sensory apparatus. These findings do not lend themselves to more precise description, because it is difficult to put into words the impression the infants conveyed. However, what the infant's body conveyed to the body of the holding person was distinct and real.

This finding deserves some comment because it seems to be an illustration of the supposition that experiences in mutual adaptation between the infant and his environment begin to influence his behavior from early infancy and are integral parts of the general learning process. In the institutionalized babies, we suggest that this failure to adapt to holding observed in the second month was already a symptom, and that the poverty of the infant's experiences in being lifted, touched, moved, cuddled, and held in the mother's arms began very early to influence his adaptation to his environment.

In the third and fourth months an interesting discrepancy occurred in the function of the lower extremities compared to the upper. The behavior of the hands and arms at this age appeared normal: the hands met in the midline and there was mutual fingering (so-called "hand play"); the eyes regarded the hands; the arms activated in rudimentary, though still mostly unsuccessful grasping efforts. The hand made connection much more reliably with the mouth in an apparently purposive manner, as one would expect. However, the lower extremities did not function in a comparably mature way: kicking activity was less than one would expect and the infant did not put his feet down voluntarily to support a fraction of his weight when placed in a standing position.

No physical or neurological findings account for this discrepancy. However, some light is shed upon this if one is willing to entertain the idea that the variety of sensory experiences that come about as a result of being touched, picked up, cuddled, and handled have something to do with the way in which an infant learns to use his muscles. We would suggest that under normal conditions of maternal care, i.e., especially with variety of sensory experiences that accompany feeding, diaper changing, and bathing, the infant is, introducing a metaphor, "energized" to use his motor abilities as they become available through neurological maturation. The fact that the hands and arms are better used than the legs at this age could be explained by the fact that a baby is able to stimulate his own hands through the hand play and hand-mouth activity that are present at this age. He is much more dependent upon another person for stimulation of the lower extremities.

We propose, then, that maternal care is one of the necessary ingredients for the optimal development of certain aspects of motor function. This hypothesis seems to be supported by findings of later months. One might ask: what are the things that a mother does to and with her baby that influence his motor behavior in particular? This has been implied in various ways when we refer to touching, moving, cuddling, etc.

Observations of family infants give a clue to this. One sees some babies whose gross motor development is delayed, while their interest in and manipulation of toys, their language, and social development are quite good. In those infants who have no motor-tract damage such a finding has occurred in our experience in two kinds of situations: one in which for various reasons physical handling is reduced to a minimum; the other in which the baby's attempts at activity are either not supported by the mother or may be actively restricted by her. The restriction may be, but is not necessarily, a punitive one. An infant who spends many hours of the day in his high chair may still have much experience with toys and good experiences in the social interchange with his mother and other persons, but his gross motor development may be delayed. For example, Tommy's gross motor development in the last months of the first year suffered from his being a "lap baby"—mother, grandmother, and father held him on their laps in a loving but not excessively exciting way to keep him off the floor. Their conscious reason was that they feared that he would either get against the hot stove or would catch a cold in the draughty room. In most respects his development was good, but there was no doubt that the prolonged restriction of his large-muscle activity at a time when he was ready to be more active resulted in a delay in standing and walking.

There are also babies in families whose motor behavior may express experiences in overstimulation from his parents. An example of this is Jerry, who had from birth been a vigorous and active baby. He crept, stood, and walked well, and was generally agile. He became hyperactive in the last part of the first year and in the second. His overactivity was maximized in situations when his mother played with him in an exciting, stimulating way. His skill in the use of his body would deteriorate under the impact of scolding or punitive behavior from her, and this regression was accompanied by a heedlessness in regard to his own safety. From a large amount of data on Jerry and his family, it could be established that his motor behavior was strongly influenced by the way in which his parents used him as a recipient of their poorly controlled libidinal and aggressive impulses (Ritvo et al., 1962).

We would suggest, then, that the kind of maternal care that especially promotes good motor development would include both physical handling and the provision of opportunities for the baby to make use of his emerging motor skills. It also requires that the physical contact between parent and child be characterized by some modicum of control in the adult of the impulses and feelings that are conveyed through touching and handling.

To return to the institutionalized infants: observations in regard to the development of head control in the institutionalized babies compared to family-reared infants are of interest. In the average baby, the ability to control his head when he is pulled from his back into the sitting position occurs between four and five months of age. In the institutionalized babies this type of head control was delayed. Interestingly, however, most of the institutionalized babies of five months or over could be "taught" within a single testing session to control the head by the procedure of repeatedly being pulled to sit in a playful way by the examiner. They seemed, after a few trials, to be able to anticipate what was about to happen, to get set, and thereby to control the head. This appears to be a clear example of the interrelationship between readiness in maturational terms and the influence of experience. The capacity to control the head in the pull-to-sit play involves not only intactness of the neuromuscular apparatus but the capacity to anticipate and respond to the actions of the adult. Thus it reflects learning as well, and is based upon experience.

[59]

The development of sitting erect, of getting into a sitting position, and of moving from a sitting position into prone was uniformly delayed in the institutionalized infants. According to McGraw (1943), there is no innate reflex sitting posture in the human infant. That this lack of an innate reflex might imply a greater dependence upon experience is a logical, though speculative idea. In any event, the institutionalized babies were delayed in this area, and the deficit in their experience included not only a specific lack of opportunities for sitting but also the deficits in being touched and handled in general.

These babies were also slow in pulling themselves into the standing position, in walking with support, and in walking alone. However, they did begin to walk in the second year, and at that time the motor development became the area in which their retardation was least apparent.

In contrast to these delays in development, there were other aspects of motor behavior which appeared normal or were only slightly retarded. Certain aspects of prone behavior were adequate. During the first six months this included lifting the head and chest from the crib mattress in the prone, visual following of an object in this position, and rolling from prone to supine. In the second six months creeping was only slightly delayed: the babies got up on hands and knees at eight and one half to nine months and soon thereafter began to creep. They did not creep very much, and there was nowhere to go, but they did creep some in their cribs, and they spent much time rocking on all fours.

Two possible explanations suggest themselves for the more adequate prone behavior. One is that the organization of the neuromotor elements involved in prone activity is extremely archaic and may be less dependent upon outside stimuli than some other gross motor activities. The second possibility is related to the infants' care in the nursery. The babies were regularly placed in prone after they were given their bottles, which means that they spent the major part of their day in this position whether asleep or awake. The visual environment of the institutionalized infants, though meager, was the major source of external stimulation. They were handled very little, and there were few sounds to listen to. Their visual preoccupation with the environment was apparent from the third month onward. It may be that the baby's visual attentiveness resulted in his expending more efforts to lift his head and look about and that these efforts contributed to the better mastery of muscle control in prone.

A discrepancy between maturation of the apparatus and its use in the infant's adaptation to his environment was seen in various aspects of the development of the institutionalized babies. It was clearly demonstrated in what happened in the grasping and manipulation of objects. The earliest grasping efforts were normal in configuration and time of appearance. Until the age of five to six months the babies would approach and grasp the toys and test materials fairly regularly, and at such times one could see that the patterns of grasp were evolving normally and that there was an adequately coordinated approach.[1] But from approximately six months on, throughout the first year this grasping behavior deviated from the norm in the following respects: one first noted at around six months that the institutionalized infant reached out for toys less frequently and the arm movements were less smoothly coordinated, although the maturational sequence was un-

[1] Gesell and Halverson (1936) and Gesell and Amatruda (1947) delineated the maturation of the grasping patterns in the infant and its sequence is included in the Gesell Developmental Examination. They develop in an orderly and predictable manner from the ulnar side of the hand to the radial side, and from palmar to digital grasping. Over the first year the normal infant develops a high degree of precision of grasp, becoming able to pick up even tiny objects with skill.

disturbed. At this time his interest in toys was less than it was earlier, and it took a longer time within a given testing session to elicit the evolving hand skills, but with patience one could establish the fact that the maturation of the grasping apparatus was proceeding in an orderly fashion. For example, the radial palmar, radial digital, and later the pincer patterns which designate the progress in thumb and index finger opposition occurred at the proper time and reflected this maturation. However, the infant did not utilize them in a normal manner in his adaptation to the environment. This is an example of a discrepancy between maturation and function; the deviant behavior here was a disturbance in the *use* of the available grasping abilities and not in their configuration.

From the age of eight to nine months there were more impressive ways in which the infant's approach to his world was distorted. The low impulse or drive to approach, grasp, and manipulate the toys was increasingly apparent. One saw several different attitudes or reactions when the toy was presented. In some infants the hands were held at shoulder height and the hands and arms appeared "frozen" and immobile. At times the arms were still while the hands and fingers trembled, waved, or moved in a manner reminiscent of the abnormal movements associated with some types of brain damage. Tentative approaches were made to the toys in which they were flicked, or picked up briefly, and promptly dropped. This type of picking up and dropping the blocks that are used in the test was designated by Gesell and Amatruda (1947) as "hot-cube behavior," a term which effectively conveys the fleeting nature of the prehension. Amatruda thought of this behavior as indicating some degree of brain damage, and if we had not seen the infants earlier—and later[2]—we would have to consider

---

[2] This behavior was reversible if the baby at this age was given adequate maternal care.

the possibility of motor-tract damage or defect. However, one could establish that the institutionalized baby did have the equipment to approach, grasp, and manipulate objects, though he put this equipment to minimal use and his movements were lacking in skill and smooth coordination.

A word must be said about the disturbance in institutionalized infants in what we have referred to as modulation of movement. In using the term "well-modulated" we wish to convey a smooth and frictionless type of motor performance appropriate to an infant's age. This modulation is usually ascribed exclusively to integration of neural centers. We would suggest that such modulation reflects more than a structural and biochemical maturation; it reflects, also, a capacity within the infant for regulating the motor impulse. It appears to require a balance between discharge of energy and inhibition of that discharge. In the institutionalized infants, especially in the second six months, the frictionless performance, the nuances and modulations of movement that would be appropriate to the age were rarely seen; the motor equipment worked mostly in "fits and starts"; there was lack of activity on the one hand or sudden, jerky, not smoothly controlled activity on the other. It paralleled the poor control of impulse that was seen in some other aspects of behavior as well. Without discounting the importance of neural integration in this balance, we believe that smooth modulation and control cannot come about in infants reared under the conditions existing for the institutional study population and that it is intimately linked to the nature of maternal care.

The normally developing infant, during the first year, is increasingly able to use his motor skills for seeking pleasure or for avoiding something unpleasant; he uses them for social interchange, for learning about the world, and for expression of his feelings. He seeks closeness to the mother, pushes her

[63]

away or hits; he comforts himself by sucking his thumb; he explores his mother's face or a toy or his own body by touching, patting, or poking. He may express excitement or eagerness by an increase in activity; discomfort or anxiety may be revealed either by an upsurge in activity or an inhibition. Anticipation may be reflected in his active search for a person or a toy that has vanished or in his expectant waiting for their return.

The institutionalized baby was strikingly different in this regard. His "movement language" was meager. The extensive repertoire of small and large movements used by the average infant by the end of the first year was not apparent. At an age when one expects to see a baby actively, specifically, and purposively directing his feelings and his interest toward the external environment through motor acts, the institutionalized baby was inactive and disinterested. It appears that all of the things he could be expected to reach out for (a toy, another person, his own body) were poorly invested. He had the equipment available to approach, seek, or cling to a potentially pleasurable situation or a comforting or loving person—but he scarcely ever did so. He also did not flee from or push away an unpleasant stimulus; in such stressful situations he could only cry in a forlorn and desolate way.

The only type of motor activity that was increased in the institutionalized infants was rocking which appeared in most of them at five to six months and by eight months was universal. It was first seen as a side-to-side head and body rocking in supine which might be pursued for fifteen or twenty minutes at a time if no one approached. Later they rocked on all fours, and still later other varieties of rocking appeared. This is described in more detail in Chapter 16 on Discovery of the Body and the Sense of Self.

In spite of the retardations and deviations in motor behavior, the institutionalized infants fared better in this respect than in other areas of development. It is not clear why this was true. It may be that intrinsic growth factors and forces came to the fore toward the end of the first year and exerted an influence that eventually resulted in the child's learning to walk alone.

Summary of Findings

In the first three to four weeks the motor behavior of the institutionalized infants was not impaired, according to our methods of observation.

The earliest deviation (second month) was a minimal capacity to make postural adjustments to being held or carried.

In the third and fourth months the discrepancy in the function of the upper and lower extremities became apparent, which suggests the importance of the sensory stimulation involved in maternal care as an "energizer" of motor function.

The control of the head in the pull-to-sit situation, the development of sitting erect, of moving from sitting to prone, and of the capacity to get oneself into a sitting position were uniformly delayed. The babies were also slow in pulling themselves to a standing position, walking with support, and in walking alone.

In contrast to the above delays, some of the motor behavior in the prone position appeared normal: lifting the head and chest from the crib mattress in prone, visual following of an object in this position, and rolling from prone to supine. Creeping was slightly delayed.

Rocking on all fours and in other positions was universal and excessive and is described more fully in Chapter 16.

A discrepancy between maturation of motor apparatus and its use in the infant's adaptation to the environment was seen in various aspects of motor function: one example is the disturbance in the grasping activity.

A diminished impulse to reach out for and move toward people and toys was easily visible from the eighth month onward and was accompanied by various unusual motility patterns.

There was a significant impairment of the ability to use the motor skills to seek pleasure, avoid unpleasure, to initiate a social interchange, to exploit the environment for learning, and to express feelings.

A disturbance in modulation of movement was increasingly apparent in the latter half of the first year.

In spite of the retardations and deviations in motor behavior, the institutionalized infants fared better in this respect than in other areas of development. They began to walk alone in the second year, and from that point onward they looked relatively best in that area of development.

Interpretations and Propositions

It is clear that the various motor functions and modes of motor behavior of an infant in his first year differ in the degree to which they are dependent upon the environment. We suggest, for example, that the institutionalized infant's poor adaptation to being held, which was observed in the second month, was a symptom that was brought about by the poverty of his experiences in being lifted, touched, and held in the mother's arms.

The disturbances in the motor behavior which reflect the nature and control of motor impulse point to another aspect of the crucial role of maternal care. Two observations are relevant: one is the infant's low impulse to approach, reach out for, and make contact with other people, his own body, and with toys. The other is the poor capacity to modulate the motor impulse to produce a smooth motor movement. If one accepts the notion that some of these are behavioral manifestations or derivatives of the psychic drives, these observations suggest a disturbance in the normal regulation and discharge of drive energy, and point to the importance of adequate maternal care in such regulation.

Our data also suggest the hypothesis that the more archaic aspects of neuromotor organization (e.g., prone behavior) are relatively less influenced by the type of deprivation that characterized the institutionalized infants than are other aspects of motor behavior. The suggestion is also made that for motor functions in which no innate reflex behavior is involved (e.g., sitting), there may be a greater dependence upon the organizing influence of the external stimulation.

The discrepancy between the maturation of the motor apparatus and its use by the infant in his adaptation to the environment is one of the principal findings of this study. It can be viewed, in terms of psychoanalytic developmental psychology, as a delay or a disturbance in bringing the various aspects of the maturing congenital apparatus under the control of the ego. It is paralleled, in the development of the institutionalized infants, by other disturbances in ego functioning.

One of the needs for stimulation is to bring the maturing systems into what we are designating as "action units." These action units are the result of a growth process combined with experience. The ability to produce a voluntary motor act as contrasted with mere motor discharge reflects the interaction of intrinsic and environmental factors. Hartmann (1939) has suggested that such an act also implies a conception of the body image at some level of awareness (see also Hartmann, 1950).

The experiences and forms of stimulation that act as the organizing and energizing influence are included in the concept of good maternal care with all that this implies. In the absence of such care, the infant's motor development suffers in certain ways. The fact that it is less impaired than some other areas of development seems compatible with Hartmann's (1939) description of motor development as one of the autonomous functions of the ego, i.e., as arising outside of conflict, from one component of the innate ego constitution. It seems to us not a contradiction to its autonomous nature to point out that at least in the first year of life motor development is dependent upon and intimately linked to the quantity and quality of maternal care.

It seems likely that at the end of the first year and the beginning of the second, endogenous maturational forces come to the fore and exert an influence that results in the infant's becoming more active motorically and learning to walk in spite of the deprivation.

13

Reactions to People, Feelings and Emotional Expressiveness

T HE DISTURBANCES in personal relationships and in emotional development have been described by many people who have studied infants reared in situations of inadequate maternal care. The terms "affect deprivation" and "emotional deprivation" have often been used to designate the deficit in the child's experiences. Chapin (1915a, 1915b), Levy (1937), and Lowrey (1940) made early contributions. Spitz (1945, 1946, 1951, 1955b, 1957, 1959, 1960; Spitz and Wolf, 1946a, 1946b, 1949) has been one of the pioneers in research into the psychogenic disorders of infancy and in the theoretical formulations of their etiology and development. Bowlby's theories on the nature of the infant's tie to the mother (1958) and on grief and mourning in infancy (1960) bring together certain ideas from psychoanalysis and ethology. Anna Freud (1960), Schur (1960), and Spitz (1960) have commented upon Bowlby's paper, and in their presentations have summarized many of the theoretical points relevant to the mother-infant relationship and to deprivation.

We will describe here in some detail a few of the many things that seem to go on between a mother and her baby and some of the responses on the infant tests designated as "social." We will compare these responses and ways of interacting with those we encountered in the institutionalized babies.

[69]

The interaction with which we are concerned can be observed from the first day of life onward, when the infant reacts to people and they react to him. One can only be impressed with the remarkable variety and increasing complexity of situations in which some contact comes about between the baby and another person. In the following pages we have referred to this person as the mother, though obviously one could also include other people who are a part of the infant's life.

The question of how something is transmitted between mother and baby is a fascinating subject about which we need to know much more. Escalòna (1953) has found it useful to distinguish between two kinds of transmissions. One she calls contagion, the other communication. She remarks that both may be one-sided and both may be mutual. By contagion she refers to "those processes whereby a feeling state transmits itself from mother to infant, as when an infant cries when held by an acutely tense and anxious person but seems quite content when held by one who is relaxed; or when a baby cries but settles down merely upon being spoken to and patted in a reassuring manner." She proposes that contagion is mediated by the various sensory modalities and is probably never fully subject to voluntary control by the person from whom it emanates, e.g., "An excited, worried mother may try to convey reassurance but the baby, if he is susceptible to contagion, will respond to her actual feeling state."

The term communication, Escalona reserves for "conscious and purposive sending and receiving of information." In this view, the behavior of the very young baby would mainly express various states of comfort and discomfort and would not be communication in the sense of purposive sending and receiving. The transitions from this expressive behavior to purposive communication occur gradually. When one can clearly observe communication it seems to reflect an important step in development because, as Escalona suggests, "it implies the baby's perception of another person as a distinct entity who responds to the self in ways that are capable of being influenced."

Other words might be used to designate these processes; it is the concept that is important. Kris in responding to Escalona's suggestion commented that one should emphasize particulary that there is a continuum of transmissions—some closer to contagion and some more in line with communication.[1]

We follow Escalona's thought that in the life of the very young baby, contagion and one-sided communications (mother to infant) make up most of the social interaction. The mother "reads" the behavior changes in the baby, attempts to judge their meaning, and acts accordingly. Her skill in interpreting the behavior, the extent to which she is attuned to his needs is, of course, dependent upon many factors which contribute to and reflect her attitudes toward him, both in a general way, and at any given moment of the day.

Escalona further suggests—and this is in agreement with our observations from work with mothers and infants—that even this one-sided communication is reciprocal as far as the emotional state of the mother and probably the baby is concerned. Even in the earliest days "when he is little more than a reactive bundle, certainly incapable of gratitude or appreciation, his behavior provides important direct gratifications to the mother." She experiences pleasure and satisfaction when the infant becomes comfortable and contented in response to something that she does for him; and if she does her best to comfort him and is unsuccessful, she may feel hurt, angry, rejected, or think she is a failure as a mother.

---

[1] A discussion remark in the presentation by Escalona (1953).

[71]

The attitudes which the mother brings to the maternal role depend on many things in her past and in her current situation, including her childhood experiences and her relation to her own parents and siblings, and to her husband (Bibring et al., 1961). The meaning of having children or of a specific child is important. There are factors of reality such as the family's financial circumstances or way of living that play a part. In addition, there are the characteristics of the child himself. For example, whether he is mature or premature, blond, brunette or redhead, active or inactive, boy or girl, healthy or unhealthy will have something to do with the attitudes she has toward him. Coleman [Lipton], Kris, and Provence (1953) have commented upon some of the variations in early parental attitudes as seen in a longitudinal study of child development.

Many, many experiences in which something happens between mother and baby are a part of his daily life. Most of his social contacts in the beginning are closely associated with his biologic needs and come about simultaneously or in close association with having those needs met.

As the first year progresses there are more exchanges with people that are at a greater distance from those needs. He learns to communicate in an increasingly clear and purposive manner, rather than being limited to an expression of his feeling state which must be identified by the mother. His relationship to her as a specific person gradually develops from what Anna Freud (1953) has called the "stomach love" of the young infant to the beginnings of love for another person. His responses to his social environment show increasing evidence of discrimination.

Some of the responses of the infant to the adult are included in the infant tests. They are those ways of behaving which

[72]

occur with sufficient frequency and regularity as to be considered "normative" behavior.

The earliest reactions (those of the first weeks) are probably of a reflex nature. For example, the infant's eyes focus and follow the adult visually in brief manner; he quiets when he is spoken to; he may frown or smile. There is no evidence that these earliest responses are accompanied by mental content. With the passage of time some of these behaviors take on new meaning, e.g., the social smile of the infant of four to six weeks differs from the "gastric smile" of the neonate, not so much in its configuration, but in the situation or context in which it occurs.

In the second and third months, the responses to people that appear on the infant tests include the responsive social smile, the infant's adaptation of his body to being held in a specific way, his vocalization in response to social stimulation from the adult, and his visual attention to a moving person. By three to four months he responds with much smiling, musical cooing, and increased body activity to social stimulation, and while his most robust responses are usually to the mother he makes all adults happy in his acceptance of them and enjoyment of the personal interchange. At the same time he is capable of strong, definite evidence of displeasure when the contact with the person is broken, as when the adult moves out of sight or sound.

Gradually there are indications that the infant discriminates between the face of a person and other things. For example, he shows a selective response to the face of the adult, as compared to a mask, between three and four months, which implies some recognition of a difference between them; between five and six months he is able to imitate some of the facial expressions of the adult.

From around four months on there are signs that he anticipates some of the things the adult does with and for him, for example, in the feeding situation (see Chapter 4). With this evidence of anticipation there are signs of a beginning capacity to wait for the pleasurable experiences. Kris (1957) speculates that this is the period when the infant's behavior suggests that "perception and memory interact to produce an anticipation of the future and the infant registers from the mother's preparation (e.g., of the food) the cues for the forthcoming satisfaction. . . ."

Other things emerge with increasing clarity in the second six months. The infant uses his voice with growing specificity to indicate feelings of pleasure, displeasure, eagerness, delight or anger. He "calls" to his mother from another room with the expectation of a response. One can see what appear to be mixed feeling states; e.g., fascination and apprehensiveness or pleasure and anxiety seem to exist side by side. More and more there are nuances of emotional behavior to be seen both in his responses to people and in his spontaneous expressions of the way he feels.

He is more active both in pursuing a social contact and in avoiding or rejecting it, and in this he uses all of the resources that are at his disposal: he utilizes his motor equipment to move toward or away from people, he smilingly invites with his eyes or he averts his gaze; he extends a toy, sometimes giving it up, sometimes pulling it back—both in the service of the social contact. He may use the toy to initiate the contact, to carry on an interchange that looks like a game of alternate giving and taking back. He can also insist on his right to have the toy by pulling it out of the adult's hand with vigor, and something that one is tempted to call assertiveness. If he is held in his mother's arms, he pokes, pats, slaps, pulls at and

[74]

fingers her various features, or he may push her away. He expresses both positive and negative feelings more clearly, and in a manner that makes the observer feel that he begins to be aware that there is some connection between what he feels and what he does. When one sees behavior such as this, one has no doubt that much of it is a conscious intentional communication, an active bid from the infant for some kind of contact with the adult.

The further development of imitative activity seen earlier in the facial mimicry is now seen in his imitation of sounds made by the adult, and some motor activities such as patting or knocking with hand or toy. The question of who imitates whom is not always clear since there is usually much imitation of the infant by the adult, which probably stimulates and enhances his imitative behavior. Spitz (1957) in particular has called attention to the importance of such interchanges in the development of the infant.

The baby first responds to, later imitates, and finally initiates such social games as peek-a-boo, pat-a-cake, and bye-bye. The response to peek-a-boo is usually seen at around eight months, the pat-a-cake and bye-bye about a month later. In the last months of the year he spontaneously repeats a performance to which the adult has given a positive affective response. This is usually a facial expression, a gesture, a sound, or a body movement, which appears to have gained its significance from the interchange between adult and baby. The signs of pleasure or excitement which accompany it are easily observable.

Alongside the increasing signs that he recognizes the mother and has formed an attachment to her as a specific person, there also occur manifestations of anxiety at her disappearance. Toward the end of the first year he is assumed to remember her for brief periods when she is absent and thus, it is believed, be partly comforted by this memory. At the same time he has a sharper reaction to separation from her, which seems to mean to him that this person who is so important can also be lost.

Concomitant with other steps in the development of the relationship between infant and mother during the first year, there has gradually developed the capacity to be interested in and to accept substitutes for the maternal figure, for example, a favorite teddy bear or blanket. It also appears that much of the infant's satisfaction with toys in general is linked to the emotional relationship with the mother. This is discussed in detail in Chapter 15 on the Reactions to the Inanimate Object.

Before presenting the findings in the institutionalized infants we want to emphasize that all degrees of adequacy of maternal care exist in families. In some instances, the care and the relationship seem to approach the optimal one as far as is known. In other instances, there are extremes of neglect or abusive treatment which have been encountered by all those who work with children. We have borrowed Winnicott's (1945) term, "the ordinary devoted mother," because it seems to convey the most frequent situation between mother and baby: namely, one in which there is reasonably good physical and psychological care most of the time, and where mothers are not too disturbed to be able to manage the maternal role fairly well. Variations in the development of infants cared for by their mothers are infinite and are the result of the wide range of possible combinations of babies with individual traits and predispositions, and mothers with their unique ways of mothering. These varieties of development in themselves are fascinating and are the subject of much important research. Babies with mothers, however, with all their variations and individuality, are still more like each other than they are like the institutionalized infants.

During the first two to three months the institutionalized

babies looked more nearly like family babies in their responses to people than they did at any later age. It is perhaps worth mentioning that they had a somewhat more frequent handling from the attendants during this early stage, as they were fed and changed more often.

The responsive smile appeared when one would expect, and they did vocalize in response to social stimulation, although even at this early age the output of sounds was diminished.

The failure to adapt in the normal way to being held was apparent as early as the second month and probably is already a symptom of the deprivation. We feel that this reaction to being held demonstrates the importance of the mother's holding, touching, cuddling, and responding even during the period when nothing like conscious awareness in the baby can be recognized. (This is described in detail in Chapter 12 on Motor Behavior.)

When one encountered the institutionalized infants at three to four months of age, one was immediately impressed with the lack of vocalizations and the intensity of their looking. The adult was looked at—even stared at—when near at hand or across the room, and the baby used all his available motor skills to keep the adult within his visual field. This visual attentiveness was such a prominent part of the infant's behavior that it was often difficult to get him to look at the test materials, and the examiner found it necessary to be as inconspicuous as possible when presenting them. The looking was accompanied by various facial expressions: sometimes the face was sober and immobile; often there was a smile; at times there was a wrinkling of the brow producing an expression that one was tempted to call puzzled. The looking, which was unusually intense and preoccupying, was the striking thing, however.

The babies continued to be visually attentive to people throughout the first year. With such an amount of looking

[77]

one might expect that the signs of visual discrimination would develop rather well, but such was not the case. The differential response to stranger vs. attendant and to face vs. mask as well as the imitation of facial expressions as measured on the tests were markedly delayed. It is of interest that their capacity to discriminate visually between the nursing bottle and other objects was much more nearly normal. It will be remembered that the infants were fed with bottle propped; the bottle unaccompanied by experiences that belong to the normal feeding situation was their primary source of relief from internal discomfort. Their familiarity with the diapering situation as indicated by appropriate body adjustment was another area in which they were only slightly slower than the average. These two experiences are precisely those that were the most often repeated in their lives.

While the institutionalized infants, in the last half of the first year, usually responded to contact with the adult with mild signs of pleasure which most often included smiling or slightly increased motor activity, they made only minimal attempts to initiate a social contact. They did not, for example, change position to reach the adult or vocalize, or even to cry in a way designed to attract attention.

In the second six months one saw no evidence of increasing personal attachment to a particular person, nor did one encounter manifestations of aggression toward others. In those infants where a more positive response to the familiar attendant than to strange examiner existed, one was still startled by the tenuousness of the tie and the minimal emotional involvement of both parties. The evidence of understanding and participation in such traditional games as peek-a-boo, pat-a-cake, and others was markedly delayed. Indeed, all varieties of playful activity which are so much a part of the interchange between mothers and babies, and which the babies continue and elaborate on their own, were underdeveloped or scarcely ever seen in the institutionalized infants.

Playful activity is an important aspect of the young child's development and promotes this development in various ways as Waelder (1932) and Greenacre (1959) have said. Waelder stressed the importance of play for the child in reducing anxiety, by its role in overcoming and mastering those situations which cause anxiety. Greenacre has pointed out that "play, being under the child's direction, can represent fragments and bits of reality according to his needs. Thus he can dose himself with larger or smaller bits of reality according to his needs and wishes." Waelder and Greenacre also accept the existence of functional pleasure in play (a term used by Karl Bühler). This refers to the sense of pleasure in performance without regard to the success of the specific activity. Greenacre relates this functional pleasure in play to a "satisfaction of maturational pressures."

In regard to the smile, it is not so easy to convey the difference in what could be seen in the smiles of the institutionalized babies, and those that one sees in family infants of the same age. The adjectives used to describe them reflect some of this. For the institutionalized babies we kept encountering in our records words such as friendly or amiable, while the smiles of family babies were described as broad, sweet, provocative, anxious, fleeting, charming, flirtatious, coy, etc. This was one manifestation of the differences in the variety of feelings and emotions that are expressed by the normal baby, as compared to the meager and constricted repertoire of the deprived baby. It is also true that there were fewer varieties of other kinds of facial expressions in the deprived babies, namely, those that in other babies we might describe as puzzled, contemplative, questioning, sad, bemused, attentive, etc.

The reaching out to pat, to caress, to scratch, to hit the face

[79]

of the adult, or to poke into the eyes, mouth, ears or nostrils was virtually nonexistent. The pleasure, excitement, anger, or exploratory interest that accompany this behavior in the normal infant were also absent. Significantly, they were unable to "defend" themselves. They did not push away the hand of the adult when something painful or unpleasant was being done to them. They reacted by crying forlornly or making half-hearted flight movements by turning the head away or moving the extremities. Only rarely did one see the child change position in order to get to or away from the adult, i.e., actively to pursue a contact or to avoid it. Most were amiable, obviously enjoyed contact with the adult, and responded promptly with a smile, mildly increased activity, or willingness to be involved in play. While their responses were bland and far from robust, they showed their pleasure in the social contact and on rare occasions initiated it. They responded with equal enjoyment to everyone who came around. A few appeared extremely depressed and subdued, smiled seldom, and the face was characteristically masklike in its lack of expression. These did not appear anxious and while they made no effort to initiate a contact, they accepted it without protest and eventually responded and looked a bit more lively.

It has been of interest to us that there was a rare infant in the institutional group who had a reaction of anxiety to the stranger of a particular kind. This was the sad-looking, depressed, sober infant who upon the approach of the stranger cried in a way that sounded anxious and distressed. The crying seemed to be entirely in response to the visual image of the stranger, and the infant stopped crying and became more comfortable when picked up and held (by the stranger) in such a position that he could not see the stranger's face. In those few babies in whom we saw this response we had hoped that it meant a better capacity for forming relationships, reasoning that if there were such accurate discrimination and anxiety to the stranger, the provision of a mother would result in a closer attachment. The follow-up of these last-mentioned babies into foster homes during the second year, however, did not support this assumption. One could see no differences in the depth of personal relationships of these children compared to those who did not have the anxiety reaction in the first year. Whether they could appropriately be thought of as having a greater predisposition to anxiety from birth, we cannot say from our data.

In the institutionalized babies, it was a consistent finding that not only was turning to the adult for play or for pleasurable contact diminished, but turning to the adult in times of distress was rarely seen. They might cry when distressed or uncomfortable (though they cried extremely little), but when they did there was no evidence that they had learned to address this expression of need to others or that they had any expectation or anticipation that the need would be met.

Summary of Findings

Earliest signs of deficit (second month) were diminished output of vocalization in response to people and a failure to adapt to holding.

The responsive (social) smile appeared at the normal time. In some, it remained for several months, while others became more sober.

There early developed a strong visual interest in the adult which persisted throughout the year. The intense looking was not accompanied by development of normal discriminatory behavior; rather, there was a poor discrimination of differences. There was a delay in signs of visual discrimination in response to the face of the adult, e.g., (a) delay in differential response to attendant vs. stranger and to face vs. mask; (b) delay in imitation of facial expressions.

There was a reversal in the usual sequence of events in that the institutionalized infants recognized the nursing bottle at an earlier age than they recognized the nurse.

The tenuousness of emotional ties was striking. There were no signs of increasing attachment to a particular person.

There was virtual absence of playful activity with others, including the social games such as pat-a-cake, peek-a-boo, etc.

The small and constricted repertoire of feelings and the impoverishment of affective expressions were conspicuous findings.

There was a general difficulty in being active, both in initiating a social contact and in warding off or avoiding an unpleasant stimulus.

The infants were characterized by amiability (with a few exceptions as described) and blandness; there was obvious, though mildly expressed pleasure in the contact with the adult.

There was an absence of anxiety to the stranger with rare exceptions as described.

The failure to turn to or to seek the adult when in distress or to solve a problem and the failure to develop a sense of trust in the adult were noteworthy. There were no signs that they anticipated or expected that a need would be met.

INTERPRETATIONS AND PROPOSITIONS

When one evaluates the observations on the institutionalized infants from the point of view of their relationships to people and the capacity for expression of feelings, one is impressed with the severity of the retardation and impairment of the emotional life. The importance of adequate nurturing and mothering in making it possible for an infant to establish a meaningful attachment to another person is obvious.

The differentiation of his affective life and the experiencing of the variety of emotions as well as the development of modes of expressing them are dependent upon this care.

The development of the capacity to play seems to be of importance as part of the child's development, both as a resource for alleviation of anxiety and as functional pleasure, i.e., the satisfaction inherent in the use of a developing function. Our data would support the view that play has its origins in the exchanges between mother and infant and derives its stimulus from the relationship. The absence of playful activity in the institutionalized infants is one illustration of how the deficit in the relationship impedes the development of an ego function that normally would be important in promoting further mastery of skills and in facilitating problem solving and the capacity to manage one's own feelings.

The observations in this study demonstrate that such developmental achievements as discriminatory responses to people, the capacity for deferring immediate gratification, memory of the past and anticipation of the future, and the building up of a sense of trust are direct reflections of the adequacy of maternal care. The capacity for initiating an action that provides a social contact or wards off danger is also absent or underdeveloped when the personal tie is tenuous.

One is reminded that many distress signals were unanswered from the earliest weeks so that the infant's opportunities for learning what and who it is that brings comfort were few. He had very few experiences of the kind that would help him to develop the awareness of some discomfort inside himself, about which he can give some signal to another person, who comes and makes him comfortable again. It is of great importance that such aspects of his care as feeding, diapering, having his position changed, or being given a toy usually occurred on an externally determined schedule, and only occasionally were related to the infant's wishes or his state of discomfort at any given moment. His experiences with discomfort and comfort were so inconsistent and fragmented that both the love relationship to another person and the differentiation of mental processes were robbed of some of their primary building blocks. For example, the mental image of a mothering person is believed to develop in the normal infant as a result of repeated experiences in which he feels his need and has it responded to by the mother. This sequence is very different in the institutionalized infants, and one would assume that the image is very dim. This idea has been further developed in a paper by Provence and Ritvo (1961) utilizing observations from this study.

14

Language

LEWIS (1959) has introduced the question about the development of language in infants as follows: "When does a child begin to learn to speak? The answer is, if not at the moment of birth, then certainly during the first day. For as soon as a child cries and some one pays attention to his cry the first step has been taken; the essentials of language are there: one person makes a sound which another person interprets." The earliest sounds are undifferentiated and nonspecific. They express some state of discomfort or comfort arising from inner or outer stimuli. Lewis traced the relationship between infants' vocalizations and states of comfort and discomfort and the emotional settings in which the advances were made. He showed that the first vocalizations emerge from and are merged with the sounds of comfort and discomfort often related to feeding. He describes what he regards as the prime conditions favorable to the growth of language: "the child is uttering sounds which are characteristics of his most vital states, and these sounds are being responded to by others in ways appropriate to those states. When he cries someone will come and feed him or relieve him of some other discomfort. When he gurgles someone will often come and smile with him and show delight in his pleasure. Gradually these satisfying experiences will become a strong incentive to him to make more and more sounds. . . ."

Vocalizations, vocal signs, gestures, words, and the comprehension of the words of others are parts of language development as it is designated on the infant tests. The antecedents of speech are the spontaneous and responsive vocalizations and vocal signals of the infant which at first have only an expressive function but increasingly become purposive communications. Some of these are indicated in the following pages.

Before he begins to vocalize in a responsive way a baby hears people talking in his presence and they also talk to him. A mother talks to her baby as she feeds, holds, lifts, changes his diaper. She speaks to him from across the room or as she bends over his crib. She responds to his earliest vocalizations as though he had used a word; she verbalizes what she assumes to be his feeling states. When she wants him to rest, she speaks softly or sings him a lullaby, accompanying this with other modes of behavior through which she tones down the outside stimulation. In other situations she stimulates him to activity and asks for a response either by speaking to him or more often by combining speech with other forms of stimulation. Not only does he hear her speak, but the expression in her voice, her tone, and the other things that accompany the words provide him with a variety of experiences that contribute to his gradual learning of the use and meaning of language.

He also hears his own voice and experiences body sensations which are part of the act of phonation. It is assumed to be important to speech development that the infant hears his own voice. A circular reaction of a reflexive nature is postulated: he vocalizes, hears himself, and thus is stimulated to vocalize further. Damage to any one segment of the pathway would therefore result in diminution of sound production. The difficulties in speech development of congenitally deaf and brain-damaged children support this idea. The structural integrity of all segments of the pathway is recognized as basic to the normal development of speech.

[86]

In addition, various authors have made reference to the importance of the environment in speech development; e.g., the observation that infants and children reared in institutions vocalize less than infants reared in families has been made by Brodbeck and Irwin (1946), Spitz and Wolf (1946a), Roudinesco and Appell (1950), and by Goldfarb (1945a). Our data support this view. We found in our study that the language behavior of the institutionalized infants was depressed by the second month, and was the area measured by tests in which improvement was slowest even after the infant had the benefit of family life.

In the normally developing family infant, the first not-crying vocalizations are throaty noises mostly resembling vowel sounds. In the second and third months there is a gradual development of a musical responsive vocalization often referred to as cooing. The family baby of this age is generous with his smile and his musical babbling to the delight of everyone. Soon he chuckles and by four months has a real "belly" laugh.

There are some aspects of normal language behavior that reflect increases in tonal range of the voice, e.g., high-pitched, squealing noises appear at four to five months, and the low-pitched noises referred to as "growling" a few weeks later. During this time the infant also begins to use his repertoire of vocalizations to initiate a social interchange with the adult. In addition, he vocalizes spontaneously when alone, as though talking to his toys or to his hands or to something else he sees.

By six to seven months there are recognizable vowel sounds and clearly enunciated consonants begin to appear. There are various vocal signs which he uses for purposes of communication. These are specific ways of vocalizing with which he communicates something in a clearly intentional way. This is no longer merely expressive; it is a communication which Escalona (1953) suggests seems to indicate an awareness of another person, separate from oneself, who can be made to respond. There is also much mutual imitation between mother and baby which includes imitation of sounds.

The vowels and consonants are combined into such sounds as mama, dada, baba, gaga by seven to eight months, but when they first appear they are not names. The mama and dada sounds and others become specifically linked to the parents and used as words during the last quarter of the first year. The process through which the nonspecific mama and dada become meaningful appears to be illustrated by the fact that parents respond to the child's vocalizations with what Escalona has called "a marvelously beneficial-kind of error." The mama and dada *become* the names for the parents because they make it so. Their interpretation of the infant's babblings, their pleasure, their strongly positive affectively charged responses to these syllables appear to be the stimulus which makes these "words" gain specificity.

This kind of transition is presumed to be an example of one way in which the response of the parent contributes to the process of differentiation in the infant's mental functioning. Their repetition, labeling, and response to the baby's reactions to his environment, his feelings, his vocalizations, etc., are very important to his recognition of himself, of other persons, and of his world. Such responses from others are essential to the development of meaningful speech.

For example, a mother talks to her baby about himself, how he feels and what he is doing; she tells him about his daddy or grandmother or brother; she identifies his actions and her own. She uses speech to convey her feelings for him. It also serves a function of communicating information to him that he only very gradually understands. Thus the mother's speech is one of the organizing influences of his mental apparatus.

[88]

By the end of the first year, again as a result of the inter-action between the maturing apparatus and the influence of the environment, the infant can imitate, in a more exact way, the words used by the adult to designate a particular object, action, or feeling. By now he has acquired all of the basic sounds he will need for future speech. He recognizes a number of everyday objects when they are named for him (e.g., light, doggie, cup, car) and has a vocabulary of two or three words besides the names of the parents. He responds to an increasing number of tones and inflections in his mother's voice in a way that indicates he differentiates the feelings behind them; e.g., he recognizes a prohibiting or scolding tone as having a dif-ferent meaning from an approving tone; he reacts differently to alarm and comfort in his mother's voice. When she says, for example, "hot" or "no-no" in a certain tone, he responds with an inhibition of activity that is clearly under voluntary con-trol.

The language development of the group of institutionalized infants was very different. They had no such language when they were a year of age. The depression in their language de-velopment was clearly discernible as early as the second month. The first signs were (1) a diminished output of sound in quan-titative terms, with or without stimulation from the adult; and (2) a lack of the full elaboration of the musical, cooing quality of the vocalization expected, at the latest, by the third month.

The nursery had an almost startling quietness. One could not escape a feeling of wonder that so little crying and so few vocalizations came from a roomful of infants. When contact was made with the individual infant through smiling, touch-ing, handling, or talking, some vocal-social responses could be elicited. In the first six months, the noises when they were heard were normal in form, but the robustness, vigor, and elaboration of sound expected at this age were lacking.

During the second half of the first year there was a continued and exaggerated depression of certain language functions, while others developed more appropriately. The infants were notably quiet and vocalized even less than they did earlier. Some could be stimulated to vocalize responsively if the examiner persisted long enough, while others remained almost completely silent throughout the period of contact (usually one to one and a half hours). There was almost no spontaneous vocalization, i.e., the use of vocalization by the child to himself and his toys, or to initiate a contact with another person. This was in sharp contrast to the variety of ways in which the average infant utilizes vocalization at this age.

At the same time, it is noteworthy that some items of language behavior as measured by the tests did appear at the expected time. It required persistent and strong stimulation to elicit these and the output was always very meager, but they could be heard. These findings included the change in tonal range of the voice (appearance of high-pitched and later low-pitched sounds) and the appearance of consonants and poly-syllabic vowel sounds which emerged (as they do in the family child) in the second part of the first year. In this we encountered a finding that was apparent in other areas of development as well; namely, a discrepancy in the institution-alized infants between the maturation and the functional use of the apparatus. In respect to language development the repertoire of sounds that the average baby uses for communication with people or for "self-entertainment" was available, but they were minimally used. This observation suggests that the maturational matrix upon which speech development depends did exist, even though the infant was virtually silent and did not use these vocalizations in any meaningful way. He might say "mama," but it was not attached to any specific

[90]

person, nor was it usually directed at a person for purposes of communication. This observation illustrates both the orderly maturation of the apparatus and the failure to make use of it in the adaptation to life. Here one has another example of the unused and unorganized potential. This poor development of speech as a function is due to the deficits in the child's experience.

⌐In the last months of the first year the language deficit was even more striking. An occasional mama or dada sound could be evoked after much effort from the adult, but these remained meaningless, nonspecific vocalizations. Altogether there was minimal vocalization of any kind. The repertoire of sounds through which the average baby by this time expresses pleasure, displeasure, anger, eagerness, anticipation, gleefulness, and excitement, or vocalizes something that sounds like a question or interjection was virtually nonexistent. None of the infants had even a single specific word by the end of the first year. Their understanding of the adult's language was also retarded, but less so than was language production.⌐

Even crying was rare and when heard was nonspecific, poorly differentiated, almost never vigorous, and lacked the variety of expression one expects to hear at this age. It fell upon the listener's ear very differently from the affect-laden cry of the family baby. There was no evidence in the crying behavior of the institutionalized baby of any anticipation or expectation that he would be responded to. This has been more fully described in Chapter 13 on Reactions to People, Feelings and Emotional Expressiveness.

SUMMARY OF FINDINGS

In the institutionalized infants speech development showed signs of maldevelopment early, became progressively worse, and was the most severely retarded of all functions that could be measured on the tests.

Earliest signs of disturbance were (a) diminished output of sounds (vocalizations of all varieties) with or without stimulation from the adult (second month), and (b) a lack of the full elaboration of the musical, cooing quality of the vocalizations.

There was continued scantiness of both responsive and spontaneous vocalization throughout the first year. The failure to develop a system of communicative vocal signals and later words was dramatic. There were no specific words at the end of the first year.

There was a discrepancy between signs of maturation of speech apparatus and the development of speech as a function. There was an emergence of changes in tonal range of the voice, in consonants and vowel sounds according to the expected biological timetable; however, these were only minimally used in the service of communication. They were not developed and organized into speech.

Language comprehension was retarded, but less so than language production.

Crying was rare, nonspecific, and poorly differentiated.

Speech development was an area that was particularly vulnerable to the conditions of the environment in which the institutionalized children lived.

INTERPRETATIONS AND PROPOSITIONS

As in other areas of development, speech comes about as a result of maturation of the neurological apparatus, stimulated and influenced in crucial ways by interaction with the environment. This is an aspect of the child's development that suffers most dramatically in a situation of maternal deprivation.

The presence and attention of the mother appear to influence the development of speech in several ways: (1) the stimulation promotes the child's own vocalizations; (2) there develops much mutual imitation which encourages the use of an ever-increasing repertoire of sounds; (3) the mother, through her way of responding to the infant in action and especially in speech, identifies or "labels" for him many things such as people, toys, himself, his feelings and actions and those of others. He comes to be able to identify many aspects of inner and outer reality because she provides the appropriate experiences; her speech is both a carrier of the emotions and an organizing influence on the infant's mental apparatus; (4) the sounds that form the building blocks for speech gain their specific meanings primarily because of the response of the parents to the infant's vocalizations; e.g., the mama and dada sounds *become* the names for the parents because of their pleasure and strong affective responses to these sounds.

The sequence of development that occurs characteristically in the speech of the institutionalized infant who at the end of the first year is placed in a family is relevant. It takes longer to see improvement in this area than in some other aspects of development and learning. The first step in recovery is marked by the appearance of single words, names of people and things and simple action verbs. As first word combinations appear they are repetitions of familiar phrases from daily life. The way in which this differs from the speech of a normally developing child is in the much longer period when the speech is predominantly used to express a need or to repeat in a literal way some phrase or sentence learned by rote or from imitation of the parent.

The vocabulary in terms of numbers of words, phrases, and sentences improves. However, it takes much longer before the children verbalize their fantasies, comment upon their play, ask questions that express a wish to learn about things or talk

[93]

about feelings. The constriction is not so much in the size of the vocabulary but in the way it is used, and as such it reflects the constriction of the thought processes and the damage to the emotional development.

In these children one can demonstrate on the tests during and after the second year a greater facility in the aspects of language that represent a concreteness of thought (e.g., ability to name objects or pictures) than in some of the speech that reflects a capacity for more abstract and flexible thought. Thus, some of the remnants of the effects of the deprivations in the first year on the mental life of the child can be detected in the characteristics of his later speech development.

Speech is one of the more complex functions characteristic of the human being. Its development can be interfered with by a variety of conditions and events. Its normal development is dependent both upon the integrity of the congenital somatic and mental apparatuses and upon certain stimulating and organizing influences in the environment. It is particularly dependent upon the presence of a maternal figure, and in the absence of adequate maternal care does not develop in the normal way. Our data illustrate the essential role of the nurturing person in the development of communication and spoken language. The personal relationship is the carrier of the variety of stimuli without which normal language development appears to be impossible.

15

Reactions to the Inanimate Object

THERE ARE many items on the infant test which involve the presentation of test materials, which we are designating here as toys or inanimate objects. Information can be obtained about some of the baby's adaptations to his environment through observing whether he perceives, manipulates, or exploits the toys which are a part of that environment. The way in which he makes use of them is also important, i.e., how the infant manipulates a toy, mouths, bites, bangs, casts, explores, combines one with another, or uses it to initiate a contact with another person. Various aspects of his perception, motor development, and general learning are revealed in these activities. The term "investment" in the toy is used here to convey an impression of the energy directed toward the toy. This is recognized in the testing situation primarily as the amount of interest and attention the infant manifests in the toy. One can describe the variations in degree of investment just as one can describe what the baby does with the toy. It is the purpose of this chapter to trace some of the major trends which can be observed in the average infant and to compare these with the institutionalized babies.

As in all other aspects of development, responses of increasing differentiation and complexity appear as the first year progresses. In the early weeks the baby responds to the toy as it comes into his line of vision, as it moves or makes a noise, or is touched, i.e., as it is brought into the circumscribed world of the young baby. Some toys are responded to more definitely or strongly than others because of such characteristics as size, motion, or sound, as well as their nearness to or distance from the infant. These responses reflect the state of maturation and integrity of the sensorimotor apparatus.

The earliest reactions, which are believed to be of reflex origin, gradually give way to more specific and differentiated behavior such as attention to the toys through visual, acoustic, and tactile senses. These are often accompanied by various types of body movement, vocalization, and changes in facial expression. By four to five months one sees the beginning ability to approach and grasp a toy in a voluntary way. The infant reacts to the familiar "cradle gym," "nursery birds," and other toys commonly suspended over the crib first by looking at them, later batting and still later grasping them voluntarily.

About the time a baby can approach and grasp in a purposeful manner, he can also take a toy to his mouth and can resecure it if it drops from his hand as long as it remains within his field of vision. By six to seven months he can do these things more easily and can also bite, transfer, bang, and wave the toy.

The infant's adaptation and learning are also indicated in other ways through the use of the toy. From seven to eight months on there are test situations which examine the infant's capacity to combine toys, i.e., to do something with two or more toys simultaneously. These and other situations in which he tries to bring two objects into some specific relationship to each other are believed to reflect capacities for integration of multiple stimuli.

One type of manipulations of toys seen during the nine- to twelve-month period has been called exploratory interest. It reflects the infant's increased attentiveness to details, and is seen in such test situations as his investigating the parts of the bell by looking closely at it and poking at its various parts with the index finger; ringing it purposively and mouthing—all done with an exploratory and an experimental flavor.

Piaget (1937) in studies of infants has described sequential steps in the development of the child's capacity to have a mental concept of the existence of the inanimate object. At first the infant reacts to the toy if it is in sight, and may fuss if it disappears, but there is no indication that he is aware that it still exists when it is out of sight. By the age of nine to ten months, however, he will begin to search for a toy that has been covered or masked, and by the end of the first year he can solve the problem of finding the toy that has been hidden from him by a solid screen. The capacity to solve this problem implies that he can now remember or have a mental concept of an inanimate object although it is out of sight.

The infant tests for the first year include several situations which indicate the progress in the infant's development of this mental concept of the inanimate object and they are of considerable interest because of the contrast between the behavior of family babies and the institutionalized babies.

In the latter part of the first year a baby also shows a developing preference for some specific toys over others. There are two types of preferred toys. The infant may develop an attachment to a toy which seems to be a specific substitute for the mother. This was designated by Winnicott (1953) as the transitional object. It may be, for example, a furry or soft animal, a doll, or a blanket. The child's apparent enjoyment of the way this object feels—its sensual character—is believed to be an important attribute because it reproduces some of the sensations of the contact with the mother. Such attachments are a part of common knowledge as illustrated by the comic-strip character, Linus and his blanket. It appears that this develops under the aegis of the mother, with the initial attachment being made possible because of the relationship with her. Later the toy seems to give some comfort in her absence and at times in her presence. It becomes for the child a beloved and important possession. In the first year one sees the beginnings of this attachment which is more prominent in the second year.

Another type of preference for one toy over another is seen from nine to ten months on, when the infant will give clear indications of choosing one toy over another, presumably because of some quality of the toy itself such as noise, detail, contour, or mouthing value. At this time if one tries to remove a toy before the infant is through with it, one often encounters a strong protest which is not alleviated by offering a substitute toy. At an earlier age he might have shown displeasure at the loss but would readily accept a substitute.

By the end of the first year a baby reflects many aspects of his intellectual, physical, and emotional growth in his contact with the toy. With toys, as in other situations, he expresses feelings of pleasure, displeasure, eagerness, satisfaction, frustration, and anger with increasing clarity as the first year proceeds. He experiments with losing and finding; he shows preferences for some toys over others. He may use a toy in the service of his contact with another person or as a temporary substitute for another person. He picks it up, drops it, creeps across the room for it, fingers, feels, mouths, bangs, or listens to it.

The deviant nature and delayed development of the behavior with toys in the institutionalized infants was another aspect of their difficulty. The earliest visual and acoustic responses as well as the early approach and grasping activity were very similar to those of the normal infant. From about four to five months on through the first year there was a decrease of investment and in the approach, grasping, and exploitation of the toys. The looking, banging, biting, feeling, shaking, sucking, fingering, poking, dropping, and picking up again, which in the average baby become more elaborate day after day, were much less prominent in the institutionalized infants. They appeared to get some pleasure from the toys, but there was never any evidence of displeasure when they were removed. No evidence of preference of one toy over another was seen in the first year, and efforts to recover a lost toy were virtually nonexistent.

Additionally, a marked delay in the development of the mental concept of the existence of the inanimate object was characteristic of each of the institutionalized babies. When a toy with which he had been playing was covered or screened, it was as though it no longer existed. He might look briefly puzzled before he turned to something else; he did not look or search for it at the age one would expect him to be able to do so. It appeared that the hidden toy either was not remembered or was not important enough to be recovered. His failure to solve the problem presented by this situation continued throughout the first year. The capacity to evaluate the situation and to persist until the problem was solved (obtain toy) was greatly impaired. We suggest that this reflects a deficit in thinking in these babies.

In general, the institutionalized infants did best with toys in those activities which they could do by imitation, after repeated demonstrations by the adult within the individual testing session. In contrast to this, they gave a particularly poor performance on test items which are believed to reflect developing integrative capacities and capacity to handle multiple stimuli. This may be of importance in some later types of thinking and problem solving.

Little spontaneous play with toys was seen in the first year when the infants were in their cribs. The play that did occur was most often a repetitive fingering or banging, with a minimal amount of elaboration, little evidence of enjoyment, and none of the experimental zest of the normal baby. It is clear that this was not the result of lack of opportunity, since some type of toy was suspended over or placed in the crib from the earliest months.

In no instance did we see one of the infants develop an attachment to a specific toy which became a comforter or "friend."

It is noteworthy that the few babies who were favorites of a particular nurse and who had more of a personal relationship also were more interested in toys.

SUMMARY OF FINDINGS

The visual and acoustic attention and responses to toys as well as the approach and grasp were very similar to those of the normal infant for the first three to four months.

From four to five months of age throughout the first year there was a decrease in investment in the toys, and in the approach, grasp, and exploitation of them.

The signs of discrimination and the capacity to make use of toys in increasingly selective and adaptive ways were poorly developed.

No displeasure at the loss of a toy was seen even when the infants appeared to get some pleasure from the toy.

No expression of preference for one toy over another was seen.

Efforts to recover a lost toy were virtually nonexistent.

There was a marked delay in the development of the mental concept of the existence of the inanimate object in the sense described by Piaget. This failure appeared to reflect at first the low investment and later also a deficit in the capacity to evaluate the situation and persist in solving the problem.

Activities with the toys that could be accomplished by imitation of the examiner were performed relatively best. In contrast, the infants gave a particularly poor performance on test items that require the use of two or more toys simultaneously.

Spontaneous play with toys was meager and tended to be repetitive and poorly elaborated. There were minimal signs of enjoyment and an absence of the experimental zest of the normal baby.

No infant developed an attachment to a specific toy as a transitional object.

It is noteworthy that the few babies who were favorites of a particular nurse and who had more of a personal relationship also had more interest in and enjoyment of toys.

INTERPRETATIONS AND PROPOSITIONS

The way in which the developing infant reacts to the toy at various ages depends, as do other functions, on the constant interaction of maturational and environmental processes. The importance of maturation of the apparatus in making possible such things as perception, manipulation, and the concept of permanence is taken for granted.

In addition, the importance of the relationship between mother and infant in influencing the reaction to the toy is supported by our material. Hartmann (1952) has indicated that "The child learns to recognize 'things' probably only in the process of forming more or less constant [human] object relationships. . . . Also the development of what one calls 'intentionality'—the child's capacity to direct himself toward something, to aim at something, in perception, attention, action. . . .—could be viewed as one ego aspect of developing object relations." Dr. Katherine M. Wolf following Hartmann's thought has emphasized that the infant's reaction to and use of toys depends in very important ways upon the relationship to people. In elucidating this concept she hypothesized that "the infant's capacity to develop a belief (a mental concept) in the consistency and constancy of the inanimate object, i.e., a world of things, is dependent upon the consistency and constancy of the human object."[1]

The suggestion that the interest of the infant in experiences with toys is built upon the relationship to the mother seems in many instances to be valid. That he invests the inanimate object with some of the feelings he has developed toward her is supported by such observations as the well-known attachment of infants to a special toy which seems to be a substitute for his mother as a source of comfort.

Some broadening of this idea seems indicated, however, and a concept which Escalona (1953) has presented seems to give an additional important point of view. She suggests that toys are "responsive" on many occasions in the sense that they move, change, or make a noise when the infant does something, and that in the earliest months he probably does not differentiate them from the human environment. However, "answers" are obtained more easily and more often from people than from things, and Escalona suggests this must be one of the facts which gradually leads the infant to make the distinction between the two. One of the most noteworthy things that the infant does not get from the toy but that he does get from the person is the emotional response.

Observations we have made in family infants who have a disturbed relationship to the mother suggest still another dimension. In order to use toys with pleasure and interest the infant appears to need both the personal attachment to the mother and some opportunity to play with toys in an atmos-

[1] Unpublished notes from Dr. Wolf's seminar on Child Development at the Yale University Child Study Center.

phere where he is not asked constantly to interact with another person; this means that the baby needs some time to himself with his toys in which he has an opportunity to exploit and use them in his own way. This is one of the experiences that provide the "detours to mastery and learning through play" which Hartmann (1939) has emphasized as an important part of adaptation. Such opportunities are present in ample amounts in the lives of most family babies, but occasionally one finds parents who, to put it simply, allow the baby no time of his own and whose ways of behaving with him minimize his opportunities of learning to gain satisfaction from play with toys. Such babies do not play with toys nearly as much or in the same way as other babies.

We emphasize the following things as important factors in the development of the child's constructive and satisfying use of toys:

1.　The personal relationship to the mother which appears to be the original source of interest in the toy and enhances it through its continued influence upon his general development. Additionally, the mother's pleasure in the baby's activity with the toy further promotes his own pleasure in the toy.

2.　The opportunity for some play with toys in an atmosphere where there is not perpetual competition from the adult. A constantly highly emotionally charged atmosphere is not, in our experience, favorable for the adaptive use of toys and of learning through play with them.

3.　The one-sided nature of the infant-toy transaction. The infant directs some of his feelings toward the toy—pleasure, anger, aggression, etc.—and the fact that there is no emotion returned helps him to distinguish more clearly between toy and person. It also provides him with materials which he can master through play and activity.

Some further formulations regarding the infant's relationship to the inanimate object and the role the mother plays in promoting the infant's development have been made by Provence and Ritvo (1961).

For the institutionalized babies in the first year there were enough toys and ample opportunities to play with them, but investment was low, and their use and exploitation of toys were deviant in ways that have been indicated.

These observations illustrate the links between the relationship to the mother and the ability to invest and make use of playthings.

16

Discovery of the Body and the
Sense of Self

THIS SECTION was suggested by some observations made upon
the institutionalized babies which set them apart in another
way from babies reared in families. The observation was that
they did much less touching, exploring, and playing with parts
of their own bodies than do babies who have adequate maternal care. There was also less thumb sucking and less genital
play. The only self-stimulating activity that was prominent
was rocking, which was excessive. Some of the forms of behavior in which an infant acts to produce some sensation within himself are designated as autoerotic. However, we are not
convinced that the self-stimulating activities observed in the
institutionalized babies should be so designated.

SELF-STIMULATING ACTIVITIES

Rocking

In the group of institutionalized infants we studied rocking
was a universal phenomenon. It was the only activity usually
characterized as autoerotic that was present to any appreciable
extent. Some began to rock as early as four to five months and
by eight months all of them rocked in one way or another. It
was usually first seen as a side-to-side rocking of head and body
when they were recumbent. When they were able to get up on

all fours they rocked back and forth in this position; after they could pull to stand they rocked from side to side. After they learned to walk (in the second year) there was some decrease in the amount of time spent in rocking, but they often returned to it when alone in their cribs.

The rocking activity of these institutionalized infants appeared to be different in some ways from that reported in the literature. The impressions gained from observing them was that they were not emotionally involved; they would rock for fifteen to twenty minutes at a time if alone, but they often looked about as they rocked, were quite ready to respond to the adult, and usually stopped rocking the moment someone approached. Behavior suggestive of excitement was extremely rare; no curve of mounting tension and discharge could be identified, in contrast to the rocking of infants reared in homes which often clearly has these characteristics. We also observed no autoaggressive component in their rocking.

Rocking is said to be the most conspicuous rhythmical autoerotic activity in infancy. Lurie (1949) reports that in an unselected sample of pediatric clinic population, one form or another of rocking or swaying was observed in 15 to 20 per cent of the population; in private practice about 10 per cent. He states that the most common time for the use of rhythmic motor patterns is when the infant is in the transition between one stage of growth and the next. For example, many infants who can get up on all fours but who cannot creep will rock in this position until creeping is mastered. Kris (1951a) in quoting Lurie adds that "the lag between one maturational step and the next can also be viewed as a frustrating experience to the child." Kris points out that the occurrence of rocking and other autoerotic activities in the face of and in reaction to frustration is well established.

Rocking is also a common occurrence in infants who have

difficulty in being motorically active from various causes: e.g., infants who do not learn to creep or walk because of a muscle disability may become rockers, especially in the latter half of the first year. It occurs often in situations in which there appears to be mounting tension either because the infant cannot utilize his musculature in a manner that would permit him to pursue his interests and hence might be a frustation, or it may occur as a response to anxiety arising from various causes.

Brody (1960) describes three types of rocking: (1) normative rocking consisting of bouncing or dancing movements which appear spontaneously in most infants and are related in time to some new achievement; (2) repetitious rocking which is self-initiated, monotonous, endures for minutes, seems to have no social function, and often leads to sleep; (3) agitated rocking which is rapid, energetic, and fatiguing. The infant is usually engrossed in the action in this last variety and seems to be beyond external influence for the time being. Brody advances several hypotheses: (1) rocking occurs in infants whose object cathexis for the mother is disproportionately intense; (2) these infants have had a relatively greater kinesthetic stimulation and have been more or less restricted in other modalities; (3) stereotypic rocking occurs in states of tension and represents the infant's attempt to re-establish bodily contact with the mother.

Rocking activity appears to be accompanied by varying degrees of emotional involvement. There may be a curve of mounting tension and discharge. In one of the groups studied by Spitz and Wolf (1949) the infants were described as having expressions which "could go to the point of orgiastic delight."

In the infants described by Anna Freud and Dorothy Burlingham (1944) in the Hampstead Nursery, rocking along with thumb sucking and masturbation were viewed as unmistakably autoerotic gratifications. The child's own body "becomes the object of its search for pleasurable sensations." These activities absorb the child's whole interest while they are enacted, and at times work themselves up toward a climax. The infants did more rocking than normal babies and at such times "the rhythmic movement of the body remains the sole occupation."

It seems reasonable to propose, when one compares the different types of rocking which have been described in infants, that this activity can be seen in at least four different forms. These forms probably have different origins and different meanings.

1. There is the transient rocking that is seen in the infant who seems to have no developmental problems in whom it appears as a rhythmic form of motor behavior in transitional periods between one stage of motor mastery and the next. As Kris (1951a) suggests, it may reflect a normal experience in frustration for the child.

2. There is the rocking, seen in the children described by Anna Freud and Burlingham and by Spitz, in which there is some degree of maternal deprivation or a disturbed relationship between mother and infant. In these infants the rocking appears to be an unmistakable autoerotic gratification in which the child seeks pleasure in his own body.

3. There is the rocking that is a prominent aspect of the behavior of the children diagnosed as suffering from the infantile psychoses. In them the rocking tends to be extremely preoccupying and difficult to interrupt and is usually a concomitant of withdrawal of outwardly directed attention or interest.

4. There is the rocking of the infants in our study which differs in some respects from all of these. It was always very easily interrupted by the approach of the adult. The fact that it appeared to be unaccompanied by excitement and had no

curve of mounting tension suggests that it had minimal value for self-comfort or gratification.

In the institutionalized babies in our group the rocking had the appearance of an automatic body activity of a primitive type, utilizing the most archaic pathways of the sensorimotor equipment. It appeared to be both undifferentiated and undifferentiating. One can speculate that it served some purpose of discharge or even of self-stimulation of a primitive and global sort, but it was difficult to see any clear differences in intensity or any evidence of self-comfort, pleasure, or satisfaction.

It may be that in these infants, the activity was devoid of evidences of excitement or pleasure because there was so little investment of the own body and that their incapacity to find pleasure in the own body was a reflection of the degree of deprivation. The deprivation in these infants was apparently more severe than in the infants of the Hampstead Nursery, most of whom had some contact with their mothers, and who also had more mothering from the nursery staff.

Spitz proposed that rocking is the only autoerotic activity that does not require a personal relationship. Our data appear to be compatible with that hypothesis.

Other Self-Stimulating Activities

As has been said earlier, all other forms of self-stimulating activity were diminished in the institutionalized babies. One way of viewing the observations is in regard to what they suggest about the infant's discovery of his own body and the part this plays in the development of the sense of self.

During the first three to four months the only striking difference from the norm was the failure to adapt to holding which has been discussed elsewhere (see Chapter 12 on Motor Behavior). Other aspects of behavior appeared normal at this

[109]

time. The sucking reflexes were intact. The looking at the hands, the hand-mouth coordination, and the hand-hand contact emerged as behavioral evidences of normal maturational progress at the same age they were seen in family infants. The hand contacted the mouth with expected frequency, and the infant sucked his fingers or thumb. The hands came together in the midline; there was hand play and mutual fingering.

A deviation from the usual behavior now appeared in that from four to five months on there was gradually less and less hand-mouth activity. Sucking of thumb or fingers with evidence of satisfaction, gratification, or relief of tension was seen very rarely. In the last half of the first year we did not observe even one infant who sucked his thumb with any frequency or the signs of satisfaction that accompany it in so many babies.

There was also, in the second six months, an appearance of poor tonus and laxity of the mouth which was usually held in a partially open attitude. Saliva trickled down the chin at frequent intervals. Toys and other objects were rarely mouthed or sucked. Concomitant with teething in the last half of the first year there was occasionally a mild increase in mouthing of toys, but the sucking, biting, and incorporative mouthing seen in most normal infants in varying intensity during this period were absent in the institutional group. These infants did not use their mouths in the variety of ways seen in family babies.

The hand play and mutual fingering which appeared in the institutionalized babies at around four months (the normal time) were not followed by the other activities in self-stimulation described for the normal infant in the first year. The hand-knee, hand-foot, foot-mouth activities, which appear in the normal infant in the four- to six-month period, were rare in the institutionalized infants. The touching of the genital area with the hand was uncommon and when it occurred, usually when the infant was nude, it seemed accidental. It was not accompanied by evidence of pleasure or excitement and was not repeated. Genital play was not seen by us, or by the attendants whom we questioned in detail about their observations. As Spitz and Wolf (1949) have pointed out, an unimpeachable study of the amount of genital play in infants would require continuous and prolonged periods of direct observation. However, we can state that there was less genital play seen in institutionalized infants than in family infants in this study using similar observational methods.

The institutionalized babies, after demonstrating that they could get thumb into mouth and after doing some thumb sucking for a few weeks, gave it up. After a beginning, this behavior withered on the vine, so to speak. The baby did not continue it as a pleasure for himself or as a comfort.

These activities which we believe both reflect and facilitate the development of the awareness of the own body either were not expressed or became attenuated in their expression.

BACKGROUND AND THEORY

The development of the sense of self as an individual, similar to but different from others, is gradual and extends over many years. Each person develops a concept of who and what he is. This concept is built up through many experiences, involves many interacting processes, and is expressed in a variety of ways. It has many facets, and first one and then another may be in the foreground of awareness at various times.

We are concerned here only with the beginnings of this very important and complicated aspect of the development of the individual.

In the developing infant it is believed that the first step in the sense of self is an increasing awareness of his own body. As the infant grows older the concept of himself as a person becomes increasingly complex, but these more complicated and differentiated aspects have their roots in the first years of life when he begins to explore and to know his own body.

The awareness of one's own body, which is also referred to as the development of the body image or body scheme, comes about as a result of a neurological process combined with experience. Schilder (1935) has emphasized that all sensations in the human are of significance in the development of the image of the own body. The sensations of the erogenous zones are believed to play a leading part as well as the sensations of the surface of the body, of the muscles and viscera. In addition, the sensations that accompany acts such as perception, grasping, moving, and sucking have an influence upon its formation. Schilder's statement suggests that maternal care is important in the infant's development of the body image. He says, "there is no question that our own activity is insufficient to build up the image of the own body. The touches of others, the interest of others in different parts of our body will be of enormous importance in the development of the postural model of the body."

In addition to the variety of stimuli that come to the infant from the environment, there are also various ways in which he produces sensations within himself. Some of these activities are referred to as autoerotic.

Studies of Anna Freud and Dorothy Burlingham (1944) have provided observations which support the view that self-stimulation arises in part as a substitute for stimulation by the mother. In the toddlers in the Hampstead Nurseries where these observations were made there was an increase in thumb sucking and masturbation when they were separated from their mothers which could be reversed when adequate substitute mothers were provided. This idea has long been taken for granted in psychoanalytic child psychology since analyses

[112]

of children demonstrated links between excessive frequency and intensity of masturbation and the absence of satisfactory relationships to parents.

Spitz and Wolf (1949) in their observations of autoerotism concluded that the freedom and moderate enjoyment that children derive from handling the genitalia in the last part of the first year and beginning of the second come from satisfactory maternal care and attention and not from any seduction or trauma. They imply that both extremes of behavior—an absence of genital play at this age as well as excessive masturbation—reflect disturbances in the mother-infant relationship. Lampl-de Groot (1950) suggests that while one may observe in normal infants "a kind of acme . . . which could be considered as an early infantile form of orgasm, perhaps the genital play is more commonly quiet and uninterrupted which leads to a diffuse kind of satisfaction."

In his discussion of early autoerotic activities, Kris (1951a) states that in order to understand these activities one must relate them to various overlapping aspects of growth. He gives an example of the merging of various factors in thumb-sucking behavior. Thumb sucking is synchronized with a maturational process, particularly with the growing capacity for purposeful motor activity. This maturational process makes the voluntary hand-to-mouth maneuver easily possible, but the thumb sucking has other implications as well. Kris calls attention to Freud's (1905) statement that the act of sucking for its own sake is independent of the nutritional act. The infant first sucks an object that is part of an external person, i.e., breast or bottle. Later he voluntarily sucks his own thumb, at times when he is hungry but also, and quite significantly, at other times as well. When a baby puts his thumb into his mouth, something happens that seems to make him more comfortable. In doing this, he begins the process of taking over from the

[113]

mother some small part of the bringing of comfort to himself or relief of tension. Additionally, his ability to use his own thumb voluntarily for this purpose implies an awareness of his own body at some level of consciousness. Thus maturational processes, the development of awareness of the own body, the nature of maternal care, and the relationship between mother and baby are all involved in the thumb-sucking behavior of the infant.

In addition to the activities designated as autoerotic, there are other modes of behavior which are acts in which the infant produces some sensation within himself. Some of these occur with such regularity and are so consistent in their expression that they appear as items on the infant tests. Others have been documented through infant observations. Some of these will be briefly presented.

It seems likely that even from the earliest days of life the eye plays an important part in the beginning of the baby's perception of himself. The visual behavior of the neonate has been the subject of a number of inquiries, among them those of McGinnis (1930), Bing-Chung Ling (1942), and Greenman (1962). The infant is visually sensitive to light from the moment of birth and his eyes briefly follow a moving object. When he is brought to the breast or when the adult's face comes within close range he often reacts by fixing his eyes upon it. Just what the infant sees in the first days of life is unknown, and there is no reason to believe that the visual images are perceived with the clarity that is apparent a few weeks later. These observations, however, do suggest that vision from the very beginning is an integral part of the way in which the infant experiences his world. Gesell et al. (1949) suggest that the eyes lead the hands in the approach to the world. Hoffer (1949, 1950) believes that while this statement "applies to a baby learning to control the outer world it does not apply to the baby learning to know its own body. . . . He learns it [his body] by touching one hand with the other hand and by touching the mouth." Greenacre (1960) postulates that "vision is not only an adjunct but an indispensable one in establishing the confluence of the body surface and promoting awareness of delimitation of the self from the non-self." It seems reasonable to assume that all of these sensory experiences contribute important components to the development of self-awareness.

When he is two and a half to three months of age a baby can look at and follow a moving object with his eyes with greater ease. He stares prolongedly at the face of the adult and very soon looks at his hands as if enchanted, appearing to watch himself as he moves his fingers.

It is interesting that he develops the ability to maintain his head in the mid-position when lying on his back at about the same time he can bring his hands together in a voluntary way and the hand play and mutual fingering are first seen. This occurs at around four months and mothers often report with considerable delight that "the baby has found his hands." In expressing this they are responding both to what looks like an act of self-discovery and the infant's pleasure in it. The advance in development of the use of the hands is probably enhanced by the finger play of the baby as well as by the mouth-hand contact. When the infant brings his hands together in mutual fingering a simultaneous experience in touching and being touched is carried out in one act. As Kris has observed, one can imagine it as a study of the limits of the self.

By four to five months the mouth-hand contact is more reliable. The infant can consistently and purposively get his hand to his mouth, and the thumb, which by now is more easily separated from the palm and fingers, can be selectively sucked.

As the ability to approach, grasp, and touch in a voluntary manner becomes easier through maturation the infant can touch other parts of his body. He reaches and feels his feet and toes by five to six months, having discovered his knees a little earlier. By six to seven months he gets his feet to his mouth and sucks upon them with signs of pleasure and enjoyment. He encounters his genital in what appears at first to be an accidental manner, and later, apparently under the concomitant influences of maturation and the sensations accompanying the touching, he repeats the act. By this time, except for his back, he can reach and stimulate all parts of his own body with his hands.

During the latter part of the first year he does many things voluntarily in which he produces some sensation within himself, and these small and repeated acts seem to reflect his growing awareness of his own body and what he can do with it. For example, he sucks his thumb, mouths his hand, fingers or gently pinches his belly or arm, tugs at his ear, tweaks his own toes, pokes into his umbilicus, pulls at his genital, strokes his cheek or lips, claps his hands, rubs his feet together, etc.

It is not possible to know precisely what the infant experiences within himself that is reflected in behavior such as that described above. There are suggestions and ideas, however, which are compatible with the observed behavior. We are particularly indebted to Escalona (1953) for her descriptions and formulations based upon careful observations of infant behavior. Part of her description of what the young infant may be imagined to experience is quoted in the following paragraphs. We present this for two reasons: (1) it seems to increase the capacity to visualize some part of what life is probably like for an infant cared for by an "ordinary devoted mother"; and (2) in their detail and richness these descriptions present a sharp contrast to the constriction, deprivation, and poverty of experience in the lives of the institutionalized babies. Escalona (1953) writes as follows:

"At first, the world is a succession of different sensations and feeling states. What varies is the quality and distribution and intensity of sensations. Except for the difference in the nature of the sensations involved, hunger, which we say originates from within, and a sharp sound or cold breeze, which we cannot imagine except as something that reaches us from the outside, are indistinguishable. There is no awareness of such things as approach [of others], withdrawal, or direction of any sort. . . . Light and darkness; harshness and softness; cold and warmth; sleep and waking; the contours of mother's face as seen from below, vis-à-vis, or even from above; being grasped and released; being moved and moving; the sight of moving people, curtains, blankets, toys; all these recede and approach and comprise the totality of experience in whatever constellation they occur at each split second in time [p. 25].
. . . As the baby's legs kick and stretch, the pressure of the diaper increases, his feet contact the blanket, gown, or end of the crib. As he flails his arms, he encounters the side of the crib, nothing, the surface on which he lies, or portions of his own body. As he is lifted, he temporarily feels the absence of contact with anything firm except the part of the body where his mother is grasping him. Simultaneously, kinesthetic sensations are quite different from before, the contours and range of his visual field change strangely as he is brought to the vertical position....
It would seem that with the oft-repeated sequence of certain muscle sensations as the baby moves an arm or leg, followed by or simultaneous with visual appearance and disappearance, or mouth contact and loss of mouth contact, the connection [i.e., between his action and its result] is established [p. 24].
[With the repetition and recurrence of these various experiences, some active, some passive, there develop what Escalona calls islands of consistency, e.g.,] A certain way of being grasped, certain kinesthetic sensations, and

[117]

the change in visual environment afforded by the vertical position combine into an awareness of being lifted, being moved, as an entity.... With the establishment of increasing numbers of situations in which the baby feels himself as either an active or passive agent of some change, *a psychological environment or awareness of the own person* [our italics] set off against something ... *not* part of the self is established as a background to all waking experience ... [pp. 25-26].

It seems to us that the importance of the ministrations of the mother in making possible those "islands of consistency" as well as in providing the variety of experiences referred to can hardly be overestimated. The details of these ministrations have been described in various other parts of the report. For emphasis we repeat that in addition to the sensory stimulation, the mother provides the organizing and integrating influence through which many kinds of perceptions become meaningful to the baby. Among other things he gradually learns who he is and who she is.

As was stated earlier, the behavior of the institutionalized infants was different from that of children reared by their mothers in respect to autoerotic activities and in other modes of behavior which we have referred to as facets of discovery of the own body and as the first steps in the concept of the self.

SUMMARY OF FINDINGS

The behavior of the institutionalized infants was impressively different from that of children reared by their mothers in respect to autoerotic activity and those other forms of behavior in which an infant acts to stimulate himself in some way.

During the first three to four months the only striking difference from the norm was the failure to adapt to holding. Other aspects of behavior such as sucking, visual attention to the hands, hand-mouth contact, and hand-hand contact appeared normal during that time.

From four to five months on the changes and deviations were dramatic. Hand-mouth contacts lessened, thumb sucking disappeared, the mouth took on an appearance of laxity and poor tonus. Toys and other objects were rarely mouthed, sucked, or chewed.

Other self-stimulating activities such as hand-foot, foot-mouth, and genital play were extremely rare. All those activities which we believe reflect as well as facilitate the development of the awareness of the body were not expressed or became attenuated in their expression. The one exception was in regard to rocking, which was characterized by an absence of signs of excitement or emotional content. It appeared to be a nonlibidinized activity in contrast to other types of rocking. The absence of autoagressive behavior further suggests a deficit in the investment of the own body and may reflect the poor demarcation of the body limits.[1] Its relevance for the understanding of the vicissitudes of the aggressive drive is not clear and suggests the need for further study.

INTERPRETATIONS AND PROPOSITIONS

These disturbances in the institutionalized group were clearly not the result of a delay in maturation in the neurological sense. Our data revealed that many of the maturational steps on which the abilities to touch, suck, and feel the various parts of the body depend appeared at the normal time. Mention has already been made of the emergence of hand-hand and hand-mouth activity which then decreased. The institutionalized infant's ability to lift his legs high in extension when he is

---

[1] Greenacre (1954) suggests, for example, that head banging may be associated in some way with a need to establish a body reality in that particular area.

[119]

lying on his back, a prerequisite for hand-foot and foot-mouth stimulation, occurred at the normal time, but he did not play with or mouth his feet. He had all the basic maturational patterns to enable him to grasp his foot, suck his thumb, play with his genital, tug his ear, touch his skin, or poke into his umbilicus, but he did these things only very rarely. The absence of this playful activity with the own body, which in the average baby is usually accompanied by some pleasure, comfort, or excitement, was most impressive. It was paralleled by the absence of playful activity or comfort-seeking with other persons and with toys, which have been described in other chapters.

The observation of the rarity of autoerotic and other self-stimulating activities (except rocking) in the institutionalized infants seems to support the idea that the ministrations of the mother are essential to the infant's awareness of his own body. The concept of adequate maternal care, as it concerns the optimal development of the body scheme, includes several factors; (1) the "dosage" of stimuli, particularly the tactile and kinesthetic; (2) the maturational phase in which the stimulation occurs, which is an important determinant of the capacity to respond in an optimal way; and (3) the emotional environment and context in which these events occur which make some experiences more influential than others. Theoretically a disturbance in any of these three factors could bring about some deviation in the development of the body scheme. In clinical practice one does see physically undamaged children with body-image problems either because of understimulation or overstimulation, which can be rather easily identified. It is less easy to identify what goes into normal development and what might be responsible for differences within the normal range. Our speculation is that some children are more optimally developed than others because of a more favorable confluence of factors: the stimulation occurs at a time of readiness in maturational terms and in an emotional climate that supports the organization and perception of the child's own body.

While we do not know what the "minimum requirements" of mothering for the development of the body scheme are, it appears that the infants in the institutional group were below that critical level. This would be compatible with the idea that one of the processes or steps in an infant's normal development is the active repetition of what he has experienced passively. In this instance, without the experience of the stimulation and interest of a mother, the institutionalized baby seemed unable to turn to his own body as an object of interest, as a source of pleasure, or for comfort. It is probably necessary for infants to experience more mothering than these babies received before autoerotic activities and other forms of self-stimulation can occur in their usual form. A similar assumption suggests itself in regard to the absence of autoaggressive activities in this group of infants.

Our hypothesis from these observations is that the institutionalized infants did not take the usual steps in self-discovery because of the deprivation of maternal care. There were not enough sensory experiences and there was not enough of a personal relationship to promote this aspect of their development. They did not demonstrate the behavior we view as reflecting and contributing to the progressive steps in the organization of the body scheme and the development of a sense of self. We assume that the body image and the sense of self are impaired in these babies. The importance of this as a reflection of a deficit in some of the early steps of ego development is apparent.

17

Differences in Vulnerability

T HE INSTITUTIONALIZED babies differed from each other in
the degree to which they were retarded, although the type of
retardation and the behavior deviations were strikingly similar in all. It was not unexpected to find that some were more
adversely affected in their development; or, to put it another
way, some infants were less vulnerable than others. The particular vulnerability of some children to the conditions of an
institutional environment has been noted by Fischer (1952).
It is common knowledge among those who know children in
institutions that some suffer more than others in their development under conditions in which their environment appears to
be the same in its main components.

There are several factors that deserve consideration in
trying to understand these differences in the institutionalized
babies. Some are related to intrinsic or equipmental factors
and others to environmental influences.

QUANTITY AND QUALITY OF PERSONAL CONTACT

First, and simplest to describe, is that the amount of stimulation from adults made a difference in the development. This
was a quantitative factor. For example, the advantage to the
baby who was nearest the work area (diapering table) was
repeatedly seen. Some interchange occurred more often between this baby and the adult. This might be no more than
a quick smile or a touch as she passed. She might say something

to him as she diapered another baby. He might have had his bottle returned more promptly if he lost it, or had his position changed more often. These brief contacts seemed to add up and to help in promoting the baby's development.

If he was also her favorite—and the nurses were understandably inclined to place the baby for whom they had special feelings nearby—another beneficial influence was added. The reasons why one infant had more appeal for a nurse than some other infant were highly individual and varied, as one would expect. The emotional communication, the amount of feeling that accompanied the handling of the favorite infant, was noticeably different. This includes a qualitative factor. The favorite babies developed more adequately than others.

MATURITY VERSUS PREMATURITY

It also made a difference whether the infant was full term or prematurely born. Although the correction factor for prematurity was always applied, the degree of retardation and the rapidity with which developmental quotients declined was greater in the premature than in the full-term babies. We were able to establish the normal endowment of the premature[1] babies and their freedom from cerebral defect or damage only after they were removed from the institution and were for several months in a family setting.[2]

It might clarify the above statement to report that under the conditions existing in the institution there was a period of time for the full-term babies between the ages of approximately three and five months, before the retardation due to

[1] A group of premature infants was studied with the same methods applied to the other infants. However, they are not included in the 75 cases of the main study reported here.

[2] A similar point was made in regard to the establishment of freedom from congenital mental subnormality of the full-term infants (see Chapter 1, note 2).

deprivation became pronounced, when it was possible to make some estimate of their endowment. During this age span the earlier reflex control over behavior has diminished and sufficient evidences of functioning of higher centers, adaptive behavior, and responses to people could be found to form an opinion as to whether or not the infant's capacities were intact. This could be determined even though there were already some symptoms of deprivation. With the premature baby no such thing occurred. It appeared that the deprivation exerted a retarding influence before the premature infant could demonstrate age-adequate test behavior in any aspect of his development. Our data indicate that the prematurely born infant was more vulnerable to prolonged deprivation than the mature infant.

THE INFLUENCE OF INBORN CHARACTERISTICS

There are innate characteristics which seemed to result in differences in the way the babies responded to the institutional environment. This is compatible with what is seen in all babies. There are differences in biological endowment; normal infants differ from each other at birth in ways that can be recognized and described, though the nature and significance of these differences is by no means fully documented or understood.

From our study we are unable to say what kind of inborn equipment is more vulnerable or more resistant to the effects of this particular environmental situation. One might speculate that an infant with strong innate impulse toward motor activity might be less retarded in his motor development than another baby whose motor drive is less strong; or that an infant whose sense organs for vision and hearing are sensitive might take in more stimulation and therefore be less deprived than another who is less perceptive. However, this was not the focus of our study and while we have a few clues, we cannot draw any conclusions. We assume that constitutional differences do help to determine the course of development of all babies including the personality development. These innate differences have been described in various ways and a few will be indicated below.

In regard to psychological development, the importance of biological forces has been emphasized particularly in psychoanalytic developmental psychology. Innate characteristics and environmental influences are recognized as codeterminants of psychic development. This refers both to the instinctual (psychic) drives and to the roots of the ego. Hartmann (1939, 1950) in particular has called attention to the importance of the inborn apparatuses (somatic and mental) in the development of the personality, and speaks of them as components of the ego constitution. The inborn apparatuses are brought successively into play through the maturational process which is largely intrinsic, though it is influenced by environmental factors. Freud proposed that the instinctual drives differ from one individual to another both in strength and in their maturation. Following Freud's thought, Alpert, Neubauer, and Weil (1956) have proposed that there are unusual variations in drive endowment which influence the course of a child's development. Individual differences in these inherent characteristics are assumed to exist.

Fries called attention to the fact that from birth some babies move more strongly and more frequently than others, and she introduced the term "congenital activity type" (see Fries and Woolf, 1953). The baby's activity seems to be one of the factors that influences his reactions to stimuli and the way in which people react to him. Thus it is one of the determinants of his general development.

[125]

Richmond and Lustman (1955) demonstrated differences in reactivity of the autonomic nervous system in newborn infants and arrived at the concept of an "inherent autonomic endowment." Lustman (1956) in a further study proposed that this endowment is one of the important determinants of the individual's psychological development.

Babies also differ from each other in such ways as their sleep patterns and in the amount of internal discomfort they seem to have when hungry. For example, even in the newborn period, one infant may be so uncomfortable in his hunger that he needs to be fed immediately, while another can be put off for a while if cuddled or talked to.

Differences in the response of babies to sights, sounds, touch, and position change have been observed, and these imply individual differences in sensitivity. It is assumed that an infant whose sense organs are very responsive to stimulation would experience the world in a different way than a less sensitive baby. It is not difficult to visualize the extremes: the difficulties in development produced by a sensory defect such as deafness or blindness are well known. At the other end of the scale there are infants with unusual sensitivities, as those reported by Bergman and Escalona (1949), who seem to be overwhelmed by the stimuli that are a part of everyday living. This unusual sensitivity is accompanied by various disturbances in their development. Between these two extremes, there is a wide range which would include most babies. The point is that each baby has his individual sensory apparatus which is one of the factors that influences the way he will develop.

There are other ways in which individual differences can be seen in newborn babies which are believed to be characteristics of their inborn equipment for development, but the above examples are sufficient to convey the point we wish to make: in all babies inborn characteristics differ and these individual characteristics or predispositions are codeterminants of their development. We assume, then, that these inherent differences would partly account for the variations in the way babies react to deficits in maternal care.

INFLUENCES OF DISABILITY, DEFECT, OR DAMAGE

The child whose equipment for development is damaged or defective in any way is especially vulnerable to the adverse influences of maternal deprivation. If he is, for example, blind, deaf, cerebral palsied, or mentally poorly endowed, he needs even more of the stimulating, organizing, and integrating influences of maternal care than does the baby who has no such handicap. This is only an underlining of what one would logically assume—i.e., if the baby does not have many resources within himself, if the apparatuses he must use in his adaptation to life do not function very well, if he has too little energy or drive, he will need even more help from others to enable him to realize his best possible development. He is less able than a nonhandicapped baby to get stimulation and experiences for himself and to organize, understand, and interpret them.

In any one of the individual institutionalized infants, the relative importance of innate endowment, degree of maturity, and adequacy of maternal care in determining his development was, of course, not possible to designate with any certainty. We believe that all these factors were of importance.

18

Teddy and Larry

A Comparison of an Institutionalized and a Family Infant

W<small>E</small> NOW present some material on two infants—one from the institution and one from a family. We knew both of these infants very well. Teddy, the institutionalized infant, had been taken into our study between the second and third weeks of life and was one of those followed longitudinally. Larry, the family infant, had been one of the infants in another longitudinal study of child development, and was known to us from the moment of birth.

The data are presented to show some comparisons and contrasts in their behavior and development. We selected Teddy because he was the best of the institutionalized group in that his developmental retardation in the first year was less severe than that of the rest of the longitudinally followed institutional group. Larry, the family baby, was by no means the best developed of the group of family babies, but an average, middle-of-the-road fellow. By selecting the best of the institutional group and an average member of the family group we hope to communicate, without danger of exaggeration, the differences in the development of infants who had adequate maternal care and those who did not.

Both infants weighed 8 lbs. at birth and were considered to

be healthy and vigorous as newborns. The comparative scores on their developmental tests for the first year are shown in Graphs 1 and 2.

Teddy, who was transferred from the hospital to the institution at age ten days was first examined by us at age twenty days. At that time he was a well-nourished, husky-looking baby who was taking adequate amounts of formula feeding. It was felt that his neuromuscular maturation was somewhat advanced; he gave the impression of particularly good maturation as judged especially by the good organization of reflex patterns, the beginning replacement of some of the neonatal reflex patterns by more mature forms of behavior, and by his visual alertness. Moreover, he was robust and vigorous looking, had a good loud cry, and his physical growth was proceeding well.

For several months, while his development showed the same kind of retardation that characterized the other infants in this setting, Teddy's performance on the tests and his general behavior and reactivity were not as severely impaired as that of the others. It has never been completely clear why Teddy did relatively better than the other institutionalized infants. However, we suggest that there are two good possibilities: (1) his inherent biological endowment may have been quite good as is suggested by the signs of good maturational progress in the earliest months; (2) he posed a problem in regard to feeding in that he frequently lost the nipple of his propped bottle and cried. Since he was endowed with a loud voice which punctured the usual quiet of the nursery, he had much more attention from the attendants. While they were not always happy with him and considered this protest something of a nuisance, it did have the result of providing more contacts with adults than other babies had in the first seven to eight months.

At the time of the examination at twenty-six weeks, Teddy

was still doing reasonably well. He was a husky, attractive infant with a moderately strong drive toward motor activity. He was able to direct his interest toward the test materials as long as the examiner was careful not to compete with the toys for his attention. His interest in the test materials at that time was greater than we encountered in the other institutionalized infants and he functioned at a higher level. There was no sign of anxiety to the stranger. He accepted the examiners with a friendly, amiable smile, and at times was active in initiating a contact by smiling or reaching toward one of us. The attendant reported that she was unable to prop his bottle as he tended to lose it from his mouth and when he did so he would yell so loudly that she had to go to him often and hold it for a few minutes. He was often placed in the small canvas bouncing chair so that he would be less noisy.

His developmental quotient on the Gesell Test was 108, on the Viennese Scale 122. The high score on the Viennese Scale was due particularly to his activity in seeking a social contact and his good motor development. However, there were some deficits in his performance on the tests when compared to the average for his age: he made no protest when a toy was removed and made no effort to recover it; he showed no signs of discriminating between familiar and unfamiliar people, nor did he discriminate between the nursing bottle and the doll. His language performance was his lowest sector and averaged six weeks below his age. He had some maturational language patterns at twenty-four weeks as revealed by the increased grunting and growling sounds and some spontaneous vocalization, but he made minimal use of vocalization in the service of the social contact. Imitative activities both in respect to facial expression and vocalizations were delayed. Grasping patterns were age adequate, but he was not as skillful in the use of his hands as the maturational pattern suggested he should be. He rocked when placed on hands and knees and in the sitting position when held on one's lap. He was described as rather stiff and not at all cuddly when held. He had some interest in motor activity and could change position by pivoting or rolling. Prone behavior was in advance of sitting behavior. There was a diminution in the amount of hand-mouth contact compared to earlier examinations. No finger or thumb sucking was seen.

Thus the impression of Teddy at twenty-six weeks (six months) was that he was doing well when compared with others in the group. However, along with the signs of favorable development, one could see beginning impairment of certain functions which was more dramatic in the last half of the first year. He was examined subsequently at thirty-two weeks, thirty-eight weeks, forty-five weeks, and fifty-five weeks, and there was a greater retardation at each examination. His decline was gradual but progressive. He became less active in his approaches to people and was not as responsive to them. His investment in toys diminished markedly and he had little or no interest in solving the problems that are appropriate to babies of his age. He was lacking in playfulness, and the impoverishment of his affective expressions was increasingly apparent. He looked less vigorous, robust, and active while maintaining an adequate weight gain. He often had a runny nose without being acutely ill. To illustrate the change, here is the description of Teddy at forty-five weeks (0;10-11).

His developmental quotient on the Gesell Test was 87; on the Viennese Scale 99. However, the decline in the test scores was not so marked as were the changes in appearance, mood, and reactions to people. Moreover, many of the things he was able to do could be elicited only transiently and after much effort on the part of the examiner.

He was solemn-faced, unsmiling, and miserable looking.

GRAPH 1

DEVELOPMENTAL QUOTIENTS—VIENNESE SCALE

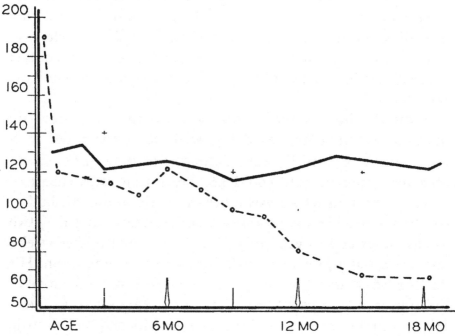

Solid line: Larry (family)
Broken line: Teddy (institution)

His nose was being wiped as the examiner approached, a measure about which he cried woefully. However, he made no effort to avoid it or to push away the nurse's hand. He was still considered by the staff a "smart little boy" compared to the others in his nursery, but he looked strikingly different from an infant in his own family. A few excerpts from a detailed observation recorded at the time are given:

> As the massed cubes are presented he looks at them, leans forward, and approaches them with his right hand. He tentatively grasps one and quickly releases it. As he fails to approach them for a time, a cube is placed in his

GRAPH 2

DEVELOPMENTAL QUOTIENTS—GESELL SCALE

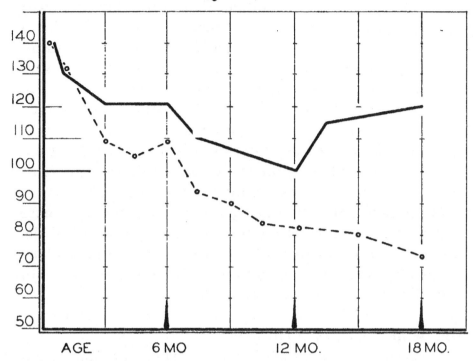

Solid line: Larry (family)
Broken line: Teddy (institution)

hand which he accepts readily. He next accepts a cube
from my hand and looks at me as though suspicious, and
finally smiles tentatively in response to my smile and my
efforts to interest him in the other cubes. He seems very
inhibited motorically as though unable to move or to
exploit anything vigorously. . . . The arms are often held
quite still in a "frozen" position which he maintains until
activated by the examiner's placement of a toy in his hand.
This is a symmetrical postural attitude in which there is a
60° flexion at the elbow, hands just above shoulder
height with palms forward; fingers are spread about 1/4
inch apart and slightly curved; thumb is partially opposed
to the palm.

[133]

He could sit, pull to stand, and could creep a few steps on all fours. He did little creeping, however, and did more rocking than creeping in this position. He could (when activated) approach and grasp the toys and had the ability to hold two simultaneously. However, he regularly discarded one, focusing his interest on a single one. He showed some displeasure when the toy was removed, but accepted substitutes easily. He made no effort to recover a hidden toy. When upset he seemed more easily comforted by being given a toy than by direct contact with the adult, including the "familiar" adult. It appeared as though having the toy in hand was more important than any attraction to the specific qualities of the toy.

His imitative responses in relation to the adult were more difficult to elicit than at the time of the last contact and the usually playful responses to social games such as peek-a-boo, pat-a-cake, so-big, etc., expected in babies of his age, were not seen. He showed no awareness of the meaning of the adult's gesture to pick him up, though he accepted the picking up with some evidences of enjoyment.

Outstanding were his soberness, his forlorn appearance, and lack of animation. The interest that he showed in the toys was mainly for holding, inspecting, and rarely mouthing. When he was unhappy he now had a cry that sounded neither demanding nor angry—just miserable—and it was usually accompanied by his beginning to rock. The capacity for protest which he had had earlier was much diminished. He did not turn to adults to relieve his distress or to involve them in a playful or pleasurable interchange. He made no demands. The active approach to the world, which had been one of the happier aspects of his earlier development, had vanished. As one made active and persistent efforts at a social interchange he became somewhat more responsive, animated, and motorically active, but lapsed into his depressed and energyless appearance when the adult became less active with him.

There were two descriptive comments by observers that seem to convey the impression Teddy made at this time. One was: "The light in Teddy has gone out"; the other was: "If you crank his motor, you can get him to go a little; he can't start on his own."

Larry, a full-term 8 lb. infant, was the second child in his family. As a newborn he was described as an attractive, husky, mature, moderately active infant, with a lusty cry. Breast-fed fully for the first six months and then gradually weaned to a cup, Larry gained weight rapidly. For the first three to four months he was somewhat fretful at night, and his mother alleviated this by holding and nursing him.

At age one month he was described as a large, well-nourished infant, who was visually alert and had the beginnings of a social smile. At age seven weeks, when first tested, he was doing well. There was some hand-mouth activity, he was visually perceptive and attentive, and responded to the adult with much smiling, cooing, and vocalizing. While he was moderately inactive as to output of movement, his movements gave the impression of strength and good organization. He adapted well to holding and reacted to being placed in the feeding position with increased sucking. His mother held him comfortably and securely. Her pleasure in him was easily visible, though she had some complaints about him.

At the twenty-week test he was socially responsive and interested in the toys. The hand-to-mouth movement was well organized and purposive. He vocalized to people and also spontaneously to toys and to himself. He played with his hands, rubbed his face, touched his body. He mouthed the toys as well as his hands. He was large, well proportioned, and moderately active.

His test performance was good, both quantitatively and qualitatively. He was smiling and attentive to the examiner, but frequently turned to his mother who sat nearby, making a visual contact and often smiling and vocalizing to her. An interchange between Larry and his mother was described by one of the observers. Part of it is included here because it demonstrates some of the differences in the experience of Teddy and Larry:

> Larry is placed on the examining table by his mother who undresses him in preparation for the physical examination; he reaches up to her face and touches it. When his shirt is removed she bends over him, rubs her nose and mouth on his abdomen and chest, nuzzling into him, kissing him and biting him gently. He chortles and gurgles with increased excitement, pulling at her hair which rubs across his nose and mouth. Dorothy, the two-year-old sister who has been playing with toys in the room, tries to get her mother's attention by calling her two or three times. Mrs. D. lifts her face briefly and with a somewhat peremptory "put the toys back" returns to her play with Larry. This play lasts perhaps two minutes, after which the pediatrician starts the physical examination. Larry, now quiet, smiles and reaches toward the pediatrician when his abdomen is palpated and gurgles as if he enjoys the stimulation.

When examined at the age of twenty-seven weeks, Larry was described as a large, well-proportioned infant who had a charming smile. His developmental quotient on the Gesell Test was 120; on the Viennese Scale 124.

There were no deficits in his performance on the test at his age level in any sector of development, and he functioned in a well-organized and well-integrated manner. He clearly distinguished between familiar and unfamiliar people and had some anxiety to the stranger. In spite of the anxiety he was able to adapt to the test situation without difficulty and became interested in and responsive to the examiner. He turned fairly often to make a brief contact with his mother, and his most intense smile was to her. His mood was a happy one.

Still partially breast-fed, he was taking solids well, including some foods from the table and some milk from a cup. He fed himself a cookie or cracker. He was up on all fours and attempting to creep. His interest in the test materials was good. He looked for a lost toy, created contact with the adult, and imitated well. He mouthed his hands and could get his feet into his mouth.

He was examined again at thirty-six, forty-three, forty-eight, and fifty-five weeks, and continued to progress well. At forty-three weeks he was a robust, vigorous infant. His developmental quotient on the Gesell Test was 103, on the Viennese Scale 114. Gross motor development was well organized at the forty-eight week level: he crept well, pulled to stand, and cruised. Moreover, he used his motor equipment effectively, either in pursuit of a toy or person, or for avoidance of an unpleasant stimulus. Fine motor skills were also well-developed. His interest in the test materials was good. He could handle two objects simultaneously with ease, showing the capacity to be interested in both and to combine objects. His general interest in inspecting and manually exploring the external world of people and things was represented in the test situation by such items as the exploratory interest in the bell which was paralleled by similar behavior toward people and toward his own body. He was aware of the relationship between the round form and the hole in the formboard and solved the problem of finding a toy behind the solid screen. He was interested in social contact with the examiner, and initiated it. He participated in such games as pat-a-cake, peek-a-boo, and bye-bye with interest and pleasure. He had a large repertoire of sounds which he used to express a variety of feeling states and used mama and dada specifically as names for his parents. He was drinking milk from a cup and was eating a variety of foods well. A brief excerpt taken from the record of Larry conveys something of the impression he made:

> He is still attractive, vigorous, and friendly, but there is a change in Larry and it is difficult to know what factors contribute to this impression. He seems more mature and less of an infant. Certainly his motor skill contributes to this as does the fact that he is less chubby and body proportions have changed somewhat. However, the predominant change is in his facial expression which is more intent, purposeful, and self-directed. . . . There is considerable mouthing and banging of toys. He bangs with large vigorous swings and seems to enjoy not only the motion but the sound. His movements are well coordinated and graceful. There is no noticeable hesitancy about approaching new objects or in giving up the old, though he looks after them and tries to retrieve them if no substitute is given. This increased interest and impression of self-directed activity is accompanied by something that makes one think he has a zest for life.

In the following months Teddy and Larry looked increasingly different from each other in their development. Their comparative scores on the two tests are given in Graphs 1 and 2. While the scores are of interest since they demonstrate some of the impact of the influence of maternal deprivation, they convey only one aspect of this influence. One was even more impressed with the differences in relationships to people and the differences in the use of the various emerging functions in the service of adaptation to people and to the everyday world of things and events. These differences, many of which cannot be expressed in a test score, also characterized the other family and institutionalized infants and have been described in the text.

PART IV

Follow-Up and Implications

19

Recovery and Follow–Up

ORIGINALLY it was not planned to include in this report the data on the institutionalized children after the first year because they are not comparable in detail and richness with the material of the seventy-five closely studied infants. However, since few institutionalized children have been followed whose infancy is known in detail, we believe that the data on their later development are relevant.

The observations to be reported here were made on a group of children that included fourteen who had been institutionalized from the first month of life. They were placed in foster homes at varying times: one as early as age nine months; one at age twenty-nine months; the others between one and two years. Four were seen one time after placement in a family; the remainder were seen from two to six times between the ages of two and five years. While the number of children reported here is relatively small, our confidence in the relevance of the observations has been supported by the fact that in the past few years we have seen many preschool children in our diagnostic service with similar histories who upon examination are found to have similar characteristics of development and behavior.

The data upon which we base this report were obtained after the children were placed in a family setting and had begun to improve. There were one or more sessions in which observations were made, tests were administered, and reports were obtained from foster parents and social workers.

Some of what will be presented are speculations and formulations and should be so regarded. We do not present this material as a definitive answer to the frequently posed question of how much impairment of later development results from this kind of experience in infancy. We have been impressed by and filled with admiration for the adaptability, resiliency, and capacity for improvement we have witnessed in the children in the course of this research. At the same time and in the same children we are just as strongly impressed with the observable and, we believe, permanent impairment of certain aspects of development; in particular we refer to the functions and capacities that reflect the more complicated aspects of adaptation, modes of thought, learning, and emotional development that uniquely characterize the human being.

We found that while there were individual variations in behavior of the children and in the rate and degree of improvement, there were certain characteristics shared by all of them. We now present the material.

Let it be recalled that these children had been in the institution since early infancy. They were placed in homes during the second year, most between 18 and 24 months. In the period between the end of the first year and the time of placement, the retardation in their development was even more impressive than in the first year and pervaded all areas that one can measure or describe.

At varying times in the second year, all learned to walk, most of them between fifteen and twenty months. They developed some kind of relationships to other toddlers in the group. These did not have the characteristics of strong or highly personal attachments, but there was initiation of and acceptance of contact with another child. This often consisted of one child's toddling up to another child's crib and handing him a shoe or a toy; two children in adjacent cribs might engage in a game of peek-a-boo. During this period most developed a few words which they occasionally used in response to some contact from those who cared for them.

They continued to be somewhat interested in adults who came into the nursery and made some distinctions between familiar and unfamiliar people, but there was less attention to persons who entered the room and less eagerness for the contact than had been characteristic of them in the first year. There was some increased investment of toys of an interesting sort: they often carried a toy around and would cry when it was removed. However, it was quite easy to stop the crying by giving another toy. The toy did not seem to be valued for the way in which it could be played with; there was very little actual play with toys, nor was there an attachment to a specific toy. The child's interest and need seemed mainly to be in having or holding the toy.

Their relationships to adults remained tenuous. Indeed, they seemed to look to the adults for certain things in the care of their bodies, i.e., feeding, bathing, diapering, wiping noses, etc., and for little else. Their emotional behavior was increasingly impoverished and predominantly bland. One saw fragments of some of the behavior expected of normal one- to two-year-olds: e.g., they might have a mild interest in exploring the environment, some degree of pleasure in the mastery of walking, and some degree of oppositional behavior—but these were pallid facsimiles of what one sees in the toddler living in his own family. One gained the impression on watching them that they had largely given up on their efforts to initiate a contact with the adult and had shifted some of the investment to the group life they led and to the possession of the toy. They lived their lives entirely in the one large room described in Chapter 3 and were uncomfortable when taken out. They reacted with more signs of upset when removed from this familiar setting (e.g., to be taken down the hall to another room) than to the presence of strangers. It appeared that the sameness of the physical environment and their presence in the group were predominant factors in their feeling of security, and that they took comfort from the situation rather than from the relationship with an adult.

This in brief was the picture they presented at the time of placement in a family. We will describe now some of the changes that occurred.

GENERAL OBSERVATIONS AND REPORTS FROM FOSTER PARENTS

In most of the children one of the first areas of improvement was in their appearance, which was even more dramatic than the quantitative gains in functioning as measured on the test. Color improved; they gained weight; their faces revealed more affect, i.e., there were more changes in expression giving clues to underlying feelings; the bland, frozen, immobile, or depressed appearance that many of them had at the time they left the institution receded. The mothers best summarized the impression of the dramatic change with the words, "He has blossomed." As a part of this change there was also a greater freedom in motor activity, more activity in initiating contact with people, and more signs of pleasure in an interpersonal contact.

The reports of the adjustment to the home were predominantly of two kinds. There were reports of an immediate and easy acceptance of the new situation with minimal or no evidence of upset. In this group there was an occasional account of a day or two of apparent apprehensiveness with either very subdued behavior or periods of crying. In the other group the shift was accompanied by more intense or more prolonged signs of upset. Some of these infants were very inactive and might just sit or sit and rock for prolonged periods and, in the mother's words, "didn't do a thing for days." Some had episodes of crying for which it was difficult to know the cause and in which it was not easy to comfort them.

During those first months, it was unusual to hear of a major feeding problem. While feeding problems were rare, the mothers did report a very interesting occurrence. Many of the children did not indicate when they had had enough to eat, and some mothers felt the children would go on eating "indefinitely" if this were not controlled. This applied both to those children who fed themselves and to those who were fed by their mothers. It appeared that they had not developed the usual knowledge of their own capacity for food; i.e., self-regulating activities in regard to food intake were poorly developed. It may be that several factors played a role: (1) the impairment of knowledge and meaning of their bodily sensations; this would appear to be one of the indicators of a disturbance in the knowledge of the own body and in the development of autonomy; (2) the difficulty in stopping to eat because it meant discontinuing a pleasurable experience; (3) the impairment of the knowledge that they would be fed again later; i.e., their difficulty in developing a sense of trust; and (4) a problem in anticipation of the future: either the anticipation of discomfort and distress as a danger, or alternatively the lack of capacity to anticipate pleasurable experiences.

Sleep disturbances were also rare. Some slept excessively and had to be waked by their mothers, or would wake spontaneously but lie quietly in the crib until someone came. Their behavior was described in terms that indicate they were docile, quiet, overly conforming, and "well trained." They were likely to follow directions (when they understood them) quite automatically and without protest. There was often an initial tentativeness about acceptance of the father, possibly because most of these children had never seen a man or heard a man's voice during their lives in the institution.

As time passed the beneficial influence of maternal care, family life, and the enrichment of experience in many areas was increasingly manifest in all aspects of development. The children became more lively, more active, began to learn to play, and to solve everyday problems. They increasingly made relationships with others. In addition, there were other signs of improvement that were not always universally recognized by the parents as signs of growth: they began now to show some provocative, negativistic, and aggressive behavior. This was a time of crisis for some of the parents and children. If the parents saw this behavior as bad or as indicating that they were failing as parents or if they felt rejected by the child, some either gave up in actuality and asked that the child be removed from the home, or withdrew some of the emotional investment and interest that were so important to his improvement. Others realized that such behavior was a necessary step in the child's progress and were able to react to it in a helpful way.

DIRECT OBSERVATIONS AND TEST PERFORMANCE

When one saw the children in the situation of the developmental examination, areas of improvement and of continued difficulty could be designated. The gains as revealed on the tests came first in areas that could be learned by repetition and rote or by imitation. For example, the imitative situations on the test involving block building, making certain types of strokes on paper with the crayon, repeating words, or imitating

[148]

motor activities were among the first to improve. The children also did well in those activities of self-feeding, dressing, and toileting in which most were quite conforming and easily taught.

Motor Development

Gross motor development in most of them was satisfactory after a few months in the family setting, although they were not graceful children and did not have smoothly flowing, well-modulated movements to the extent seen in family children. They did make use of their motor skills much more adequately than before for the pleasure in activity, for overcoming obstacles, and for moving toward or away from people or toys. The motor system in this way expressed an improvement in certain aspects of ego functioning. One did encounter some remnants of the earlier motor behavior at times: under the impact of excitement or when the child was eager to have or do something, one often saw a tremor of the hands, or some mild breakdown in the coordination of body movements.

Along with the dramatic improvement, there were characteristics and areas of difficulty which appear to be the result of the earlier experiences. These are briefly summarized below.

Language

Language development was the first area to be depressed in early infancy and remained the sector of greatest retardation as measured by the tests during the period of institutional living. It also took a longer period of family living for significant improvement to take place. When the child, in the family setting, began to use language he learned first single words, as one would expect, and then short phrases. There were no permanent disturbances in articulation of particular sounds attributable to the institutional experience. Some of the children clung to infantile pronunciations excessively long, but no true dysarthria was noted. There was a prolongation of the period of mimicking or repeating the words of the adult and a delay in the child's spontaneous verbalizations. The child tended to use certain learned phrases related to his needs and routine matters of everyday life without elaborating these for a much longer time than the usual family child. This paralleled and also reflected a certain literalness and concreteness of thought, which are described later. Gradually he began to use pronouns and to combine words to make sentences. He could talk to an adult and to other children. The use of language for asking questions and expressing ideas and fantasies and verbalizing feelings came very slowly and was not as well developed as that of the family child at a comparable age.

Reactions to People

The child's way of relating to the adults (examiner and mother) in the test situation was another characteristic finding. It was rare to see a child who had lived as much as 18 months in the institution turn to the adult for help in solving a problem. This is in contrast to the common behavior of the family child of this age who if interested in the situation will ask for help when he needs it or will seek comfort or reassurance from the adult when he feels disturbed or frustrated by the task. The deprived child was highly unlikely to do either of these things. Much more common was the observation that when he worked for a time at the task and was not successful he left it as though disinterested and looked for something else or pushed it aside with some expression of impatience. If the problem involved was in getting something he very much wanted such as a cookie or candy, he might persist in trying to solve it and if unsuccessful might begin to cry or fret or go off into a corner alone. Only rarely did he make a direct bid to the

[150]

adult for help with the problem. The adult did not seem to be viewed as one who would help him in this kind of situation.

In addition, while there was some turning to the mother for comfort when the child was upset, it was much less frequent than occurs in the family child. These institutionalized children did not seem to see the adult as a comforter or protector or as a person who makes things right. In a stressful situation, some would seek the mother, but more often one saw the forms of behavior that were reminiscent of the first year: they might cry—sometimes loudly, sometimes sadly and dolefully—or stand silently with head lowered, looking frozen and miserable. They might rock or suck their tongues or occasionally a finger or thumb.

The point we wish to make is that even after many months with the same mother and much improvement, the utilization of the relationship as a source of comfort, of relief from tension or as a source of help in problem solving remained significantly impaired when compared to the child who has had adequate maternal care from the beginning.

Another characteristic of the developing interpersonal relationship was that the child was likely to appear to be indiscriminately friendly. The relationship to others seemed superficial. In many of the children this had a definite sequence: it was not unusual in the first months of the attachment to the mother that the child seemed fearful when taken out of the house and might also be upset if the mother went out. We have assumed that the preference for the mother was a healthy sign and that it indicated some growth of relationship and some recognition of the importance of the mother. However, after this initial period of a few months it was a very common occurrence that the child became quite friendly to everyone. Though he recognized the parents as familiar and important people, he was much too ready to accept other individuals.

[151]

Such children are often very attractive to adults at first because they initiate a social contact, smile, and are friendly, and do not seem shy or fearful. They do not show the amount of caution, reticence or fear toward the strange adult characteristic of other young children. Later the adult might become disappointed when the relationship failed to deepen on further contact. We believe that this reflects a lack of depth and specificity in the relationship, and is comparable in the preschool child to Goldfarb's (1943b) findings of a superficiality of relationships in adolescents who had inadequate parental care in the early years.

With our children, it was usually very easy for one adult to substitute for another in the care of the child as long as the immediate need was met. It appeared that the personal attachments were at a very immature level and that the child remained related predominantly to the mothering process or activity. This is a level of emotional relationship that would conform to Anna Freud's (1954) description of one of the normal stages of relationship in which it is possible to exchange the nurturing person as long as the child's need is met. The normally developing child gradually develops from this stage in which the relationship is to the need-satisfying object to a more mature personal relationship in which mother (and others) become increasingly important as specific individuals. In the two- to five-year-olds who have been deprived, the relationship to others, even after months and years in the same home, suggested some degree of impairment of the capacity to develop the more mature form of emotional tie.

Problems of Control of Impulse and the Capacity to Defer Gratification

Some degree of difficulty in the control and modulation of impulse and in the capacity to defer immediate gratification of needs was characteristic of all the two- to five-year-olds in the institutional group and appears to indicate some residual impairment in their development. After some months in a family setting and apparently as a result of good maternal care, the child increasingly expressed his feelings, needs, and wishes in ways that could be recognized. There was a shift from the passivity, depression, and lack of energy and interest that characterized him earlier. One saw feelings of pleasure, excitement, love, and anger assert themselves. However, one also observed that the child's ability to modulate and control them was impaired. This statement does not overlook the fact that all children in this age group have their troubles with the development of impulse control. We are concerned here with the greater difficulty seen in the institutionalized child when compared to a family child who has had good care. These observations support the view that the capacity to control impulses is dependent upon good parental care and that the normal child in a family gradually builds up this capacity out of a complicated combination of experiences of gratification and frustration that are a part of his relationship to his parents.

In addition, the capacity to defer or postpone immediate gratification of needs was impaired in the group of institutionalized children. It appeared that with the improvement in care and the developing relationship to a mother, they became aware of and able to express their needs and wishes. However, it was very hard for them to wait for what they wanted with any assurance that the need would be met, or to give up the wish in return for approval by the mother.

To illustrate some of the behavior that characterized the children with these problems, we cite two examples from our records.

1. This time Mary Ann (age thirty-seven months) showed much more interest in the test materials and

found it difficult to wait for them to be given to her. When a toy was placed before her on the table she reached for it immediately and was so intent on having it that she was not able to stop and pay attention to what was requested of her. Her mother said she is always in a hurry, impatient, and does not want to take time to do things. She had great difficulty in deferring immediate gratification or in proceeding slowly to solve a problem. One had the impression with some of the problem-solving items that if she could have controlled her impulse to grasp the material long enough to stop and look at it more closely, she might have done better.

2. When the test materials were presented to Tommy (age forty-five months) he could hardly wait until he was permitted to have them. He seemed so eager to handle them that he was not able to listen to what the examiner wanted him to do, and if the materials did not "behave" fairly immediately for him, he became impatient and could not work at solving the problem. When his first attempts were not successful he was left with no resources. His performance with the formboard was typical: he was able to insert the three blocks in the formboard, but when it was rotated he picked up the blocks immediately and tried to force them into the wrong holes. It was not possible to get him to stop and look and re-evaluate. Later with the ball play he could not control his impulse to throw the ball immediately when he got it or to chase it pell-mell across the room and could not pay attention to the examiner's directions about what to do with it. When there was something he wanted to do he was not able to wait and when there was something he wanted he simply couldn't bear not having it. The inability to defer gratification and the impulsiveness seemed to interfere seriously with his learning generally.

The difficulty in learning related to the problem of deferring gratification and postponing discharge demonstrates some of the complex interrelationships of the developmental process. The capacity to think, i.e., to interpose a thought process between the stimulus and an act, is dependent upon the individual's capacity to delay or inhibit the discharge of the impulse; this capacity was impaired in the group of institutionalized children and is reflected in a learning difficulty.

Difficulty in Making Transitions

The difficulty in making transitions was another observation from the test situation which characterized the previously deprived child. It will be recalled that in the second year in the institution we had seen considerable crying and signs of upset when the children were shifted from their familiar room to other places. In the two- to five-year-olds seen after many months of family life one continued to recognize some problem reminiscent of this. It appeared as a diminished capacity to shift from one situation, activity, or thought to another and suggested some lack of flexibility in the mental life and in the capacity for adaptation to change. One gained the distinct impression of some rigidity both in the thought process and in the personality structure. One might speculate that it reflected a constriction in the number of adaptive and defensive maneuvers available to the child's ego.

Impairment of Thinking

A few other types of problems or tasks introduced by the tests with which the institutionalized children had more difficulty than with some other forms of learning are indicated below:

1. Problems in Thinking Through and in Anticipation

On the test there are some tasks the solution of which depends upon the child's capacity to "think through" a situation. Such problems impose upon the child the necessity to traverse in his own mind the various possibilities for solution and to find the correct one. The solutions depend, at least in part, upon the capacity to defer discharge and thus to think, as

[155]

described earlier, and also upon the capacity to anticipate the future. The child must be able to think in a logical and sequential manner about problems appropriate to his age and stage of mental development.

2. Problems in Generalizing

The test presents the child with some tasks which might be solved by generalization from one situation to another. An example of this in these children would be the following: They have "learned" by imitating the examiner in the test situation to remove a ball or cookie from a high table, using a stick to take it off; and they could repeat this once they learned it. However, they have not been able to remove a different ball from a different table using a different stick. This and similar observations suggested that the ability to generalize as one aspect of the thinking process was disturbed for much longer than some other mental functions.

3. Difficulty in Overcoming Obstacles

This is partly a repetition of what has been said earlier. When confronted with an obstacle in the test situation the family child usually attempts to solve the problem by attacking or overcoming the obstacle or turning to the adult for assistance. Our institutionalized children were much less effective in their mastery of such situations. This probably is determined by several factors: (1) the problem in thinking and anticipating referred to earlier; (2) a lower investment or capacity to persist in problem solving generally; and (3) the lessened awareness of the adult as a helping person who might be employed to assist the child.

4. Excessive Concreteness of Thought

In the developing mental life of the average child concrete learning and modes of thought precede and are essential steps in the development of more abstract learning and thought processes. The failure to progress normally, or the impairment of this development, is often designated as "excessive" concreteness of thought and has been described in various conditions. For example, adults and children with certain types of brain damage and with psychotic types of disorders are often so characterized.

The institutionalized children also had some tendencies in this direction. Although it was by no means as marked as in the above disorders, one did encounter in them some concreteness of thought and rigidity beyond what one expects in the average family child of the same age. It expressed itself in the literalness with which they responded to questions, in some difficulty in dealing readily with tasks requiring capacities to abstract, and in the failure to elaborate their ideas. Some of their perseverative behavior seemed to reflect this problem. It was also characteristic of them that there was impoverishment or impairment of the capacity to imagine, which could be seen in their play, in conversation, and in responses to questions.

This characteristic of concreteness is not likely to give rise to complaints from their teachers since much of the progress in school especially in the early years places a premium upon learning by memory and rote, at which many of these children do reasonably well. However, when it comes to seeking alternate solutions, to generalizing, and to the development of some kind of originality or creativity in thinking, one has the impression that they do much less well. This goes along with a constriction in the variety of adaptations they are able to make, and would be considered a sign of some impairment of ego functioning.

[157]

Summary

The infants who had shown the retardation and disturbed development in the first twelve to eighteen months described in the major part of this report made dramatic gains when given the benefit of good maternal care and family life. In many aspects of their development they looked sufficiently improved that they were not markedly different from their peers on superficial observation and casual contact.

However, when one looked more closely one could recognize certain characteristics which appear to be related to the absence of adequate maternal care with all that this implies. The areas in which there were residual impairments of mild to severe degree were in their capacity for forming emotional relationships, in aspects of control and modulation of impulse, and in areas of thinking and learning that reflect multiple adaptive and defensive capacities and the development of flexibility in thought and action. A lessened capacity for the enjoyment and elaboration of play and an impairment of imagination were also evident. One missed in them the characteristic of the healthy family child of richness and originality in the personality in which one perpetually discovers or catches glimpses of some new facet.

20

Implications and Practical Applications

I N THIS report the similarities and differences in the behavior of infants living in an institution and in families have been presented. The retardation and deviations in behavior, development, and learning in the group of institutionalized infants have been designated and have been compared with a group cared for by parents.

We have described the environment in which the institutionalized infants lived largely from the point of view of what the babies experienced in their day-to-day living, and have compared their experience with that of family babies.

We have given in some detail what seem to be important aspects of the many things that are included in the concept of adequate maternal care. This has been done mainly through comparing and contrasting the experiences, development, and characteristics of the two groups of infants.

At the end of the first year of life the institutionalized infants who were studied were different in many ways from the babies reared in a family environment. The general impairment of their relationships to people and the weakness of the emotional attachment were prominent abnormalities in their development and behavior. They rarely turned to the adult for help, comfort, or pleasure. There were no signs of a strong attachment to any one person, nor any signs of the development of a sense of trust in the adults who cared for them. The capacity for anticipation of the future and the ability to defer immediate gratification of needs were impaired.

The retardation of speech and the meagerness of all forms of communication were striking. They used no words, had no names for people or objects, and used very few vocal signals to express a feeling or to indicate a need. Their play with toys was impoverished, poorly elaborated, and repetitive; it lacked the signs of pleasure, interest, and experimental zest seen in the family babies. Some aspects of their motor behavior were delayed or deviant, although in this area they looked relatively better than in other functions.

Their behavior did not indicate the normal development of a sense of self. They seemed to have a low investment not only in all aspects of the environment but in themselves as well. They did not turn to such autoerotic activities as thumb sucking or genital play, although all rocked excessively. They had difficulty in being active either in order to make a contact to obtain comfort or pleasure or in order to avoid an unpleasant situation. They appeared virtually defenseless when faced with a painful stimulus.

There were indications in various aspects of their behavior that the maturation of the apparatus, as a neurological process, had proceeded in a normal manner, and yet they were unable to make use of the maturing systems in their adaptation to life; development failed to progress normally although the basic endowment was normal.

In contrast to this picture, a baby who has adequate maternal care develops much and learns many things in the first year of his life. By the time he is a year of age he is upright and interested in walking; he has a spoken language and a vocabulary of two or three words; he can communicate his wants and feelings in a variety of ways. He recognizes his mother as a person of special importance, can remember her for a brief time in her absence, and expresses his personal attachment to her. He has learned to know also a few other people whom he may accept as a substitute for the mother for brief periods of time. He enjoys various kinds of playthings and uses them for pleasure, for learning, and for expression of his feelings. While he is still quite dependent upon others for many things, he has already developed ways of doing some things for himself, of being active about mastering anxiety, of solving simple problems, and at times of comforting himself when he is upset. He has some awareness of himself as distinct from others; he has a "provisionally organized personality."[1]

All of these aspects of his development can be thought of both as accomplishments of the first year of life and as the foundation upon which later learning is built. In this respect our findings are compatible with those of Hebb (1949) who stresses the importance to later learning of the learning experiences of infancy. In the normal infant one can observe not only many evidences of learning and the mastery of certain skills and developmental tasks, but also the beginnings of an ability to adapt to new experiences and to approach new problems. In this he utilizes and is influenced by previous learning and past experiences. Some of these first steps in learning might be thought of as the infant's learning how to learn.

Hartmann (1939) has pointed out that one of the characteristics of the human being is that he has to acquire, through learning, many of the processes by which he adapts to life and to his environment. In the institutionalized baby the steps through which he learns how to learn as well as his mastery of the developmental tasks of the first year were disturbed and distorted. These observations support the supposition that many aspects of learning and modes of adaptation observable in the normally developing infant are intimately linked to and dependent upon maternal care.

One of the central hypotheses of the study is that adequate

---

[1] A term introduced by Anna Freud (1953).

development and learning in the first year come about through an interaction of the infant's inborn maturing systems and the forces of the environment. One of the needs of the baby is that the maturing systems be organized into "action units" in order that they can emerge as functions and be used in his adaptation. Our data reveal that in many aspects of development this organization does not occur in the absence of the variety of stimuli and communications that are a part of mothering. The most important aspect of the infant's environment in his first year is adequate maternal care with all that this implies.

The study reported here supports the view that severe deprivation of maternal care has an adverse effect upon the development of infants. It also illustrates that human development, even in infancy, is complex and multidetermined. The effects of maternal deprivation on an infant in the first year of life depend upon the degree of deficit in both the quantity and quality of maternal care, upon the infant's biological endowment, and upon his age and the length of time he is subjected to the deprivation. Many individual combinations of these factors are possible and produce a variety of clinical pictures in terms of severity of symptoms. The variations in the clinical picture appear to have resulted in some confusion in developing a systematic and vigorous approach to the prevention and treatment of the disorder.

There are at least two questions which have been raised repeatedly: (1) to what extent are the effects of prolonged maternal deprivation reversible by placement in a family setting, and (2) what is the maximum length of time an infant can tolerate maternal deprivation without suffering permanent damage to his personality development? The answers to these questions are important, but they are not answered by this study. Moreover, because of the complex problems involved in studying them, it is unlikely that specific answers

[162]

will be found in the near future.[2] It is well established that great improvement occurs when the institutionalized infant is placed in a situation where good care is provided. Some aspects of the development of infants placed in a family, after twelve to eighteen months in the institution, have been indicated in Chapter 19 entitled Recovery and Follow-up. While such improvement is dramatic and gratifying to the observers, it does not provide the answer to either of the questions posed above. It does not guarantee complete recovery, and it places the emphasis on treatment, the outcome of which is unknown. We believe that a much greater emphasis should be placed upon prevention, and therefore it appears both appropriate and essential to utilize, as adequately as possible, what is known about the adverse influence of maternal deprivation in the first year.

There is a need for wider recognition of and emphasis upon the importance of the first year of life in the personality development of the individual. The infant is most dependent upon others in this year of his life, his needs for nurturing are greatest, and he has least well-developed resources for withstanding the effects of the failure to meet those needs. The deficits in the experience of the infant who has little mothering are reflected in the impoverishment of his relationships to people and in retardation of many aspects of his development. The symptoms increase in severity as the period of deprivation lengthens. They are more pervasive and involve more aspects of his behavior and development if he suffers the deprivation during the first year of his life than if it should occur at a later time.

Time is of paramount importance in the life of an infant. In the life of an adult a six-month period slips by quickly, and

[2] Ainsworth's (1962) recent review of the difficulties of research in this area summarizes the problems very well.

it represents only a small fraction of his life and experience. For an infant in his first year in a situation of inadequate care it is of far greater relevance. It represents many lost opportunities for learning, for doing, and for getting to know and becoming attached to another person. There are too many points of delay in making plans for babies. Months pass while an infant's legal status remains unsettled, while his parents are unable to decide whether to keep him or release him for adoption; while there is no social worker who can help to make a plan for him, or while he waits for a foster or adoptive home.

It must be recognized that there is no magic in a home per se. The homes, both adoptive and foster, must be selected with skill, so they will provide at least reasonably adequate care for the needs of infants.

Adoptive home placement is an important approach in providing maternal care as early as possible. The need for a permanent home early in the child's life cannot be overemphasized. The trend toward adoptive placements in the early weeks of life is increasing and has many advantages both for the infant and for the adoptive parents. In order to make appropriate plans for early placement, agencies must have enough well-trained workers (1) to help the baby's mother arrive at a decision that is appropriate for her and for the baby; (2) to select adoptive homes and prepare the prospective parents for early placement; and (3) to be able to individualize their practices enough to provide adequate maternal care for the infants when early placement for some reason cannot be effected.

There is a need for more foster homes for infants who for any reason have been separated from their mothers and yet are not available for adoption. To provide adequate care the substitute parents must have enough interest in the child to care for him in a way that meets his needs as far as possible. It is essential to maintain the quality of foster-home care at a high level. This can be facilitated (1) by providing meaningful supervisory help when it is needed; (2) by recognition of the importance of the role of the foster parents; and (3) by adequate financial support to make it possible for them to continue. The contribution of foster parents to the present and the future of the child cannot be measured in dollars and cents, but without adequate financial support agencies cannot provide enough foster homes to meet the need.

Realistically, one must assume that institutions for infants will continue to serve a function not yet possible to fulfill in other ways. While they cannot duplicate the good home in the quality of maternal care, they need not be places in which an infant is damaged. They can be used in a constructive way as a temporary living situation, if they are adequately staffed and the staff includes people who understand some of the basic needs of infants—and these include, as our study convincingly shows, more than good physical care. We want to emphasize again that the infants in this study were meticulously cared for physically. But there must be more care and more personalized care for each baby. This can be effected (1) by an increase in the total number of persons available to care directly for the infants. It is both inhuman and unrealistic to expect that one person could provide anything like adequate maternal care for ten to twenty babies. Staff can be increased both by having more personnel and by the use of volunteers; (2) by an increase in the amount of time devoted to the care of every baby; (3) by a decrease in the number of different individuals caring for each baby. This requires that each of the staff members in the institutions take care of only a few babies, and that they care for the same babies day after day. They must have enough time to devote to them so that they can provide both the amount of care and the personal interest that are of such importance.

[165]

The implementation of a program designed to prevent the adverse effects of maternal deprivation requires support from the general public and from the various professional people involved—social workers, physicians, nurses, lawyers, legislators, and from the individuals and boards that set the policies of institutions, public health agencies and social agencies. It will involve changes in legal procedures; it will require greater numbers and better trained child-care workers, and a shift in cultural attitudes toward infants and children without families. Financial support while essential is not sufficient in itself to effect the changes that are considered necessary to provide better care for infants.

Appendices

Appendix A

Notes on Validity of Tests of Institutionalized Infants

The Gesell Developmental Examination and the Hetzer-Wolf Baby Test from the Viennese Scale were the infant tests used in the examination of the babies. The use of the tests in this study, as well as some of the thinking about the use of infant tests in general, has been described in Chapter 2.

A particular point in regard to the interpretation of test scores is relevant. It is a characteristic of both of the baby tests used in this study that the developmental quotients tend to be lower after the first three to four months of life. In full-term, healthy infants, living in their own families, test scores of 140 to 160 are not unusual in the first three to four months, while scores of 100 to 120 are more characteristic of the second half of the first year. Thus, the highest scores on infant tests are often, though not always, obtained during the first three months of life after which they usually, though again not always, decline. One of the criticisms of the work of Spitz voiced by Pinneau (1955) was that he did not take this into account in considering the significance of the tests in his studies on hospitalism. In order to evaluate this point, we tested a group of 75 foster-home infants[1] during the first year who had always lived in a family setting. Their scores were compared with the 75 institutionalized infants. This comparison, which is shown in Table I and in Graph 3, demonstrates that the decline in D.Q. scores of the institutionalized infants is significantly greater than that of infants in families. It was not possible to

[1] This is a different group from the family infants with whom the institutionalized infants are compared elsewhere.

[169]

match the two groups in any rigorous way as to genetic background. However, they were all children born out of wedlock and the mothers of the institutionalized and foster-home groups came from comparable racial and socioeconomic backgrounds. The early placement of the infants in foster homes was a matter of the policy and activity of the child-placement agencies involved and was not related to the characteristics of the infants themselves.

In the group of institutionalized infants we studied the major findings in regard to the test scores can be summarized as follows:

1.   Retardation in the developmental age or general maturity level, expressed as the developmental quotient, was progressive throughout the first year. During the first three months most of these infants had scores which were adequate when one computed the average value. The scores of most of them fell below 100 for the first time on the test scale between the fourth and fifth months. However, even in the earliest months when they were at their best, the D.Q. scores for this group were significantly lower than the scores of infants living in families.

2.   Not only did the developmental quotient drop during the second and third trimesters of the first year, but the differences between the D.Q.s of institutionalized infants and the family infants with whom they were compared became progressively wider.

3.   There were individual differences in the rate of decline in the institutionalized infants just as there are individual differences in the scores within a group of normal infants. This finding is compatible with the general expectation of differences in innate endowment. We have felt it important, however, not to overlook other factors that can play a part in this variation. These are discussed in the text in Chapter 17.

COMPARATIVE SCORES ON GESELL TESTS

	Number of Cases	Mean D.Q.		
		14-26 wk.	27-39	40-52
Instit.	75	101	87	85
Family (Foster Home)	75	111	108	106

	Median D.Q.			Range of D.Q.		
	14-26 wk.	27-39	40-52	14-26 wk.	27-39	40-52
Inst.	102	92	84	83-125	72-107	72-92
Fam.	116	108	107	99-151	91-126	95-112

Graph 3 presents the same scores graphically.

GRAPH 3

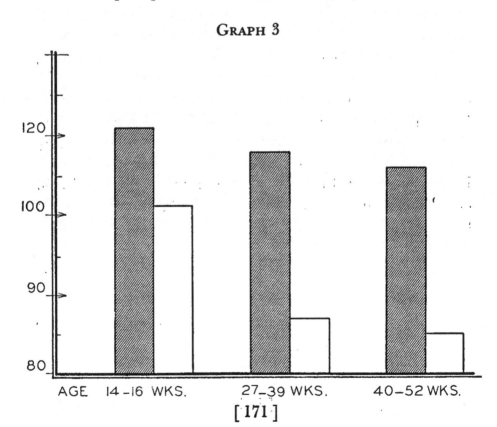

Appendix B

Summary of Test Patterns in Institutionalized Infants

The most significant finding in respect to the test performance of the institutionalized babies was that there was a remarkable and to us unexpected consistency in respect to the individual items passed and failed on the tests. While there were differences in degree of retardation mentioned above, the specific deficits in test performances were uniform and followed the same pattern in all infants. This has been described in the text and is summarized in condensed form below. The items are divided into four large categories of behavior: Motor, Language, Responses to People, and Responses to Toys. Within each category there is simply a listing in three columns: (1) test items in which there was little or no retardation, (2) test items in which there was retardation varying from mild to severe, and (3) a listing of unusual or deviant behavior not covered by the standardized test items. The lists should be read from above downward and the items are recorded in chronological sequence.

MOTOR BEHAVIOR

	No Retardation	Retardation	Unusual or Deviant Behavior
0 mo.	Reflex responses	Kicking activity	Failure to adapt to holding
	Arm activation	Support of weight on lower extremities	
	Hand engagement		
	Rolling: prone to supine		
		Head control: pull to sit	Rocking (excessive)
	Emergence of hand-to-mouth maneuver	Rolling: supine to prone	Disappearance of thumb sucking
	Maturation of grasping patterns	Foot play (hand-foot; foot-mouth)	Absence of self-touching
	Lifting legs high in extension (supine)	Sitting erect	Decreasing skill in coordination of movements
	Head control in prone	Changing position: sitting to prone and back; pivoting	Unusual motility patterns: hand waving, hand posturing, "athetoid" movements
		Reaching out to people, toys	
		Creeping (mild retardation)	Inhibition of movement
		Pulling to stand	Poor modulation of movement (poor modulation of motor impulse discharge)
12 mo.		Walking	

[173]

LANGUAGE BEHAVIOR

	No Retardation	*Retardation*	*Unusual or Deviant Behavior*
0 mo.	Early ah, eh, uh sounds	Cooing	
	Emergence of vowel sounds	Vocal social responses Chuckling & laughing	Quietness
	Emergence of consonants	Spontaneous vocalization to toys, self, to adult	
	Changes in tonal range of voice (high pitch, low pitch, etc.)	Use of voice to initiate social contact	
		Differentiation of vocal signs (pleasure, eagerness, recognition, displeasure, anxiety, etc.)	
		Use of language for communication	
		Specificity of mama, dada words	
12 mo.		Understanding verbalizations of others	Discrepancy between maturation and function

RESPONSES TO PEOPLE

	No Retardation	Retardation	Unusual or Deviant Behavior
0 mo.	Visual attentiveness	See also Motor and Language Behavior	Intensity of visual regard of adult
	Responsive smile	Recognition of nurse	
	Spontaneous smile	Discrimination of face vs. mask	Failure to establish a personal attachment: tenuousness of emotional ties
		Reflection of facial mimic	
		Anxiety to the stranger	
		Participation in social games (peek-a-boo, pat-a-cake, etc.)	Failure to seek out the adult either for pleasure or when in distress
		Initiation of social games	
12 mo.		Reaching out to adult to touch, caress, explore or act aggressively	

The test scores alone tell only a fragment of the story. Some of the most important and most characteristic facets of an infant's development cannot be expressed quantitatively in the present state of our knowledge. While the major effort of

RESPONSES TO TOYS (INANIMATE OBJECTS)

	No Retardation	Retardation	Unusual or Deviant Behavior
0 mo.	Visual and acoustic attention Early grasping efforts		
		Memory for hidden toy	Decreasing interest in toys
			Rarity of spontaneous play with toys
		Investigatory behavior	Rarity of mouthing of toys and other objects
		Combining of toys	
		Simultaneous attention to two or more toys	
		Preference for one toy over another	
		Recovering toy when obstacle is introduced	
12 mo.			Absence of transitional object

our report is to convey as many of those other traits as possible, we well recognize the gap between the words, however exact they try to be, and the impact of the personal experience with an impoverished infant.

[176]

Bibliography

AINSWORTH, M. (1962), The Effects of Maternal Deprivation: A Review of Findings and Controversy in the Context of Research Strategy. In: *Deprivation of Maternal Care: A Reassessment of Its Effects.* Geneva: World Health Organization, Public Health Papers 14, pp. 97-159.

ALPERT, A., NEUBAUER, P. G., & WEIL, A. P. (1956), Unusual Variations in Drive Endowment. *The Psychoanalytic Study of the Child,* 11:125-163. New York: International Universities Press.

BAKWIN, H. (1942), Loneliness in Infants. *American Journal Diseases of Children.* 63:30-40.

——— (1949), Emotional Deprivation in Infants. *Journal of Pediatrics.* 35:512-521.

BAYLEY, N. (1933), Mental Growth During the First Three Years. *Genetic Psychology Monographs,* 14:1-92.

——— (1940), Mental Growth in Young Children. *Yearbook of the National Society for the Study of Education,* 39:11-47.

——— (1949), Consistency and Variability in the Growth of Intelligence from Birth to Eighteen Years. *Journal of Genetic Psychology,* 75:165-196.

BENEDEK, T. (1938), Adaptation to Reality in Early Infancy. *Psychoanalytic Quarterly,* 7:200-214.

BERGMAN, P. & ESCALONA, S. K. (1949), Unusual Sensitivities in Very Young Children. *The Psychoanalytic Study of the Child,* 3/4: 333-352. New York: International Universities Press.

BIBRING, G. L., ET AL. (1961), A Study of the Psychological Processes in Pregnancy and of the Earliest Mother-Child Relationship. *The Psychoanalytic Study of the Child,* 16:9-72. New York: International Universities Press.

BOWLBY, J. (1951), *Maternal Care and Mental Health.* Geneva: World Health Organization Monograph No. 2.

——— (1958), The Nature of the Child's Tie to His Mother. *International Journal of Psycho-Analysis,* 39:350-373.

[177]

————— (1960), Grief and Mourning in Infancy and Early Childhood. *The Psychoanalytic Study of the Child*, 15:9-52. New York: International Universities Press.

BRODBECK, A. J. & IRWIN, O. C., (1946), The Speech Behavior of Infants Without Families. *Child Development*, 17:145-156.

BRODY, S. (1956), *Patterns of Mothering*. New York: International Universities Press.

————— (1960), Self-Rocking in Infancy. *Journal of the American Psychoanalytic Association*, 8:464-491.

CHAPIN, H. D. (1915a), A Plea for Accurate Statistics in Infants' Institutions. *Archives of Pediatrics*, 32:724-726.

————— (1915b), Are Institutions for Infants Necessary? *Journal American Medical Association*, 64:1-3.

COLEMAN [LIPTON], R. W., KRIS, E., & PROVENCE, S. (1953), The Study of Variations of Early Parental Attitudes: A Preliminary Report. *The Psychoanalytic Study of the Child*, 8:20-47. New York: International Universities Press.

————— & PROVENCE, S. (1957), Environmental Retardation (Hospitalism) in Infants Living in Families. *Pediatrics*. 11:285-292.

ERIKSON, E. H. (1950a), *Childhood and Society*. New York: Norton.

————— (1950b), Growth and Crises of the Healthy Personality. In: *Symposium on the Healthy Personality*, Supplement II; Problems of Infancy and Childhood, ed. M. J. E. Senn. New York: Josiah Macy, Jr. Foundation.

————— (1959), *Identity and the Life Cycle* [*Psychological Issues*, Vol. 1, No. 1]. New York: International Universities Press.

ESCALONA, S. K. (1950), The Use of Infant Tests for Predictive Purposes. *Bulletin of Menninger Clinic*, 14:117-128.

————— (1953), Emotional Development in the First Year of Life. In: *Problems of Infancy and Childhood*, ed. M. J. E. Senn. New York: Josiah Macy, Jr. Foundation.

————— & HEIDER, G. (1959), *Prediction and Outcome*. New York: Basic Books.

————— & LEITCH, M., ET AL. (1953), *Earliest Phases of Personality Development; A Non-Normative Study of Infant Behavior* [Monographs of the Society for Research in Child Development, Vol. XVII, Serial No. 54, No. 1, 1952]. Evanston, Ill.: Child Development Publications.

—— & MORIARTY, A. (1961), Prediction of Schoolage Intelligence from Infant Tests. *Child Development*, 32:597-605.

FISCHER, L. (1952), Hospitalism in Six-Month-Old Infants. *American Journal of Orthopsychiatry*, 22:522-533.

FREUD, A. (1952), The Mutual Influences in the Development of Ego and Id. *The Psychoanalytic Study of the Child*, 7:42-50. New York: International Universities Press.

—— (1953), Some Remarks on Infant Observation. *The Psychoanalytic Study of the Child*, 8:9-19. New York: International Universities Press.

—— (1954), Psychoanalysis and Education. *The Psychoanalytic Study of the Child*, 9:9-15. New York: International Universities Press.

—— (1960), Discussion of Dr. John Bowlby's Paper. *The Psychoanalytic Study of the Child*, 15:53-62. New York: International Universities Press.

—— & BURLINGHAM, D. (1944), *Infants Without Families*. New York: International Universities Press.

FREUD, S. (1905), *Three Contributions to the Theory of Sexuality*. London: Imago Publishing Company, 1949.

FRIES, M. E. & WOOLF, P. J. (1953), Some Hypotheses on the Role of the Congenital Activity Type in Personality Development. *The Psychoanalytic Study of the Child*, 8:48-62. New York: International Universities Press.

GESELL, A. & AMATRUDA, C. (1947), *Developmental Diagnosis*, 2nd ed. New York: Hoeber.

—— & HALVERSON, H. (1936), Development of Thumb Opposition in the Human Infant. *Journal of Genetic Psychology*, 48:339-361.

—— ILG, F. & BULLIS, G. (1949), *Vision: Its Development in Infant and Child*. New York: Hoeber.

GOLDFARB, W. (1943a), Infant Rearing and Problem Behavior. *American Journal of Orthopsychiatry*, 13:249-265.

—— (1943b), The Effects of Early Institutional Care on Adolescent Personality. *Journal of Experimental Education*, 12:106-129.

[179]

———— (1945a), Effects of Psychological Deprivation in Infancy and Subsequent Stimulation. *American Journal of Psychiatry*, 102:18-33.

———— (1945b), Psychological Privation in Infancy and Subsequent Adjustment. *American Journal of Orthopsychiatry*, 15:247-255.

GREENACRE, P. (1954), In: Problems of Infantile Neurosis: A Discussion. *The Psychoanalytic Study of the Child*, 9:16-71. New York: International Universities Press.

———— (1959), Play in Relation to Creative Imagination. *The Psychoanalytic Study of the Child*, 14:61-80. New York: International Universities Press.

———— (1960), Considerations Regarding the Parent-Infant Relationship. *International Journal of Psycho-Analysis*, 41:571-584.

GREENMAN, G. (1962), Visual Behavior of Neonates (to be published).

HARTMANN, H. (1939), *Ego Psychology and the Problem of Adaptation*. New York: International Universities Press, 1958.

———— (1950), Comments on the Psychoanalytic Theory of the Ego. *The Psychoanalytic Study of the Child*, 5:74-96. New York: International Universities Press.

———— (1952), The Mutual Influences in the Development of Ego and Id. *The Psychoanalytic Study of the Child*, 7:9-30. New York: International Universities Press.

———— KRIS, E., & LOEWENSTEIN, R. M. (1951), Some Psychoanalytic Comments on "Culture and Personality." In: *Psychoanalysis and Culture*, ed. C. B. Wilbur & W. Muensterberger. New York: International Universities Press, pp. 3-31.

HEBB, D. O. (1949), *The Organization of Behavior*. New York: John Wiley.

HOFFER, W. (1949), Mouth, Hand, and Ego-Integration. *The Psychoanalytic Study of the Child*, 3/4:49-56. New York: International Universities Press.

———— (1950), Development of the Body Ego. *The Psychoanalytic*

Study of the Child, 5:18-23. New York: International Universities Press.

KRIS, E. (1951a), Some Comments and Observations on Early Autoerotic Activities. *The Psychoanalytic Study of the Child*, 6:95-116. New York: International Universities Press.

———— (1951b), Opening Remarks on Psychoanalytic Child Psychology. *The Psychoanalytic Study of the Child*, 6:9-17. New York: International Universities Press.

———— (1957), Unpublished Report from the Longitudinal Study of Personality Development. New Haven: Yale Child Study Center.

LAMPL-DE GROOT, J. (1950), On Masturbation and Its Influence on General Development. *The Psychoanalytic Study of the Child*, 5:153-174. New York: International Universities Press.

LEVY, D. (1937), Primary Affect Hunger. *American Journal of Psychiatry*, 94:643.

LEVY, R. J. (1947), Effects of Institutional vs. Boarding Home Care on Infants. *Journal of Personality*, 15:233.

LEWIS, M. M. (1959), *How Children Learn to Speak*. New York: Basic Books.

LING, BING-CHUNG (1942), A Genetic Study of Sustained Visual Fixation and Associated Behavior in the Human Infants from Birth to Six Months. *Journal of Genetic Psychology*, 61: 227-277.

LOWREY, L. G. (1940), Personality Distortion and Early Institutional Care. *American Journal of Orthopsychiatry*, 10:576-585.

LURIE, R. S. (1949), The Role of Rhythmic Patterns in Childhood. *American Journal of Psychiatry*, 105: 630-660.

LUSTMAN, S. (1956), Rudiments of the Ego. *The Psychoanalytic Study of the Child*, 11:89-98. New York: International Universities Press.

McGINNIS, J. M. (1930), Eye Movements and Optic Nystagmus in Early Infancy. *Genetic Psychology Monographs*, 8:321-427.

McGRAW, M. B. (1943), *The Neuromuscular Maturation of the Human Infant*. New York: Columbia University Press.

PIAGET, J. (1937), *The Origins of Intelligence in Children*. New York: International Universities Press, 1952.

PINNEAU, S. R. (1955), The Infantile Disorders of Hospitalism and Anaclitic Depression. *Psychological Bulletin*, 52:429-453.

PROVENCE, S. & RITVO, S. (1961), Effects of Deprivation on Institutionalized Infants: Disturbances in Development of Relationship to Inanimate Objects. *The Psychoanalytic Study of the Child*, 16:189-205. New York: International Universities Press.

RHEINGOLD, H. L. (1956), *The Modification of Social Responsiveness in Institutionalized Babies* [Monographs of the Society for Research in Child Development, Vol. XXI, Serial No. 63, No. 2]. Evanston, Ill.: Child Development Publications.

RIBBLE, M. (1943), *The Rights of Infants*. New York: Columbia University Press.

RICHMOND, J. & LUSTMAN, S. (1955), Autonomic Function in the Neonate: Implications for Psychosomatic Theory. *Psychosomatic Medicine*, 17:269-275.

RITVO, S., ET AL. (1962), Some Relations of Constitution, Environment, and Personality As Observed in a Longitudinal Study of Child Development: Case Report (to be published).

ROUDINESCO, I. & APPELL, G. (1950), Les répercussions de la stabulation hospitalière sur le développement psychomoteur des jeunes enfants. *La Semaine des Hopitaux* (Paris), 26:2271-2273.

SCHILDER, P. (1935), *The Image and Appearance of the Human Body*. New York: International Universities Press, 1950.

SCHUR, M. (1960), Discussion of Dr. John Bowlby's Paper. *The Psychoanalytic Study of the Child*, 15:63-85. New York: International Universities Press.

SPITZ, R. A. (1945), Hospitalism: An Inquiry into the Genesis of Psychiatric Conditions in Early Childhood. *The Psychoanalytic Study of the Child*, 1:53-74. New York: International Universities Press.

—— (1946), Hospitalism: A Follow-up Report. *The Psychoanalytic Study of the Child*, 2:113-117. New York: International Universities Press.

—— (1951), The Psychogenic Diseases in Infancy: An Attempt at Their Etiologic Classification. *The Psychoanalytic Study of the Child*, 6:255-275. New York: International Universities Press.

—— (1955a), The Primal Cavity: A Contribution to the Genesis of Perception. *The Psychoanalytic Study of the Child*, 10:215-240. New York: International Universities Press.

—— (1955b), Some Factors in the Etiology of Psychogenic Diseases in Infancy. *Proceedings of the 3rd Annual Psychiatric Institute*, Sept. 21, 1955 at the New Jersey Neuro-Psychiatric Institute, Princeton; pp. 60-68.

—— (1957), *No and Yes: On the Beginnings of Human Communication.* New York: International Universities Press.

—— (1959), *A Genetic Field Theory of Ego Formation.* New York: International Universities Press.

—— (1960), Discussion of Dr. Bowlby's Paper. *The Psychoanalytic Study of the Child*, 15:85-94. New York: International Universities Press.

—— & WOLF, K. M. (1946a), Anaclitic Depression: An Inquiry into the Genesis of Psychiatric Conditions in Early Childhood. *The Psychoanalytic Study of the Child*, 2:313-342. New York: International Universities Press.

—— —— (1946b), The Smiling Response: A Contribution to the Ontogenesis of Social Relations. *Genetic Psychology Monographs*, 34:57-125.

—— —— (1949), Autoerotism: Some Empirical Findings and Hypotheses on Three of Its Manifestations in the First Year of Life. *The Psychoanalytic Study of the Child*, 3/4: 85-120. New York: International Universities Press.

STONE, J. & CHURCH, J. (1957), *Childhood and Adolescence.* New York: Random House.

WAELDER, R. (1932), The Psychoanalytical Theory of Play. *Psychoanalytic Quarterly*, 2:208-224, 1933.

WINNICOTT, D. W. (1945), Primitive Emotional Development. *Collected Papers*. New York: Basic Books, 1958.

—— (1953), Transitional Objects and Transitional Phenomena. *International Journal of Psycho-Analysis*, 34:89-97.

—— (1957), *The Child and the Outside World*. New York: Basic Books.

Index

INDEX

Masturbation *(continued)*
in institutionalized infants, 111
see also Genital play
Maternal attitudes, 72
Maternal care (family infants)
and autoerotic activities, 112-114
and body image, 112
and learning, 161-162
and motor development, 56-59, 62, 65-68
and reactions to people, emotions, 73-74
and response to toys, 95-98, 101-104
and self-awareness, 113-118, 120-121
and self-stimulation, 111-118
and speech, 87-89
review of literature, 3-4
Maturation
and body image, 121
and development, 12, 16
and development of motor apparatus, 57-68
and equipment, 17
and psychological development, 125
and reaction to toys, 96, 101
and self-stimulating activities, 106, 113, 116, 119
and speech, 89-91, 92-93
defined, 20
Mental apparatus, 88-89, 93
Mental image
of hidden toy, 97
of mother, 84
of self, 121
Mental subnormality, 7, 123
Metabolic disorders, 12
Methodology, 3-22
design of this study, 5-8
Moriarty, A., 10, 179
Mother-child relationship, disturbed
and body-image problem, 121
and motor development, 58-59
and use of toys, 102-103
Mother-infant interaction
and reaction to toys, 101-104
and rocking, 107-108
and speech, 86-89, 92-93

mutual adaptation, 37-38, 69-76, 78-79, 88
see also Maternal care, Mutuality
Motor activity
experiences with, 48
output, 55-56
see also Motor behavior
Motor behavior
after foster home placement, 146, 149
and failure to adapt to holding, 109
and relationship to people, 74-75
deprivation and, 77, 181
influence of over- and understimulation, 58-59
in second year, 144-145
of family infants, 58-59, 63-64
of institutionalized infants, 55-58
summary of test patterns in institutionalized infants, 173
Motor disability and rocking, 107
Mouth, in institutionalized infants, 110-111, 118-119
Movement
abnormal, 62
"language," 64
modulation of, 63-66
Mutuality, 69-76, 88; *see also* Mother-infant interaction

Negativistic behavior after foster home placement, 148
Neubauer, P. G., 125, 177
Neurological abnormality, diagnosis of, 7
Neurological examination, use in this study, 5-8
Neurological status
postural adjustment, 56
reflex behavior, 56-57
tonus, 56
see Brain damage; Mental subnormality

Object relationship; *see* Relationship to people

[189]

Date Due

Due	Returned	Due	Returned
4-30-64 (R.D.)			
MAY 2 '64 ML(D)	JUN 1 0 '64		
NOV 2 5 '64	NOV 20		
JUN - 8 '65	OCT 4 '65 ML		
OCT 1 2 '65	NOV 22 '65		
DEC 2 - '65	DEC 8		
DEC 1 5 '65	DEC - 7 '65 ML		
OCT - 5 '66	SEP 27 '66		
NOV 1 4 '66 ML	NOV 1 4 '66 ER		
JAN 2 0 '67 ML	JAN 31 '67		
NOV 26 '67	RE 2 '67	RE RE	
FEB 11 '68	RE FEB 13 '68		
MAY 1 1 '68 RE	MAY 8 - '68 RE		

Made in the USA
Middletown, DE
03 February 2023

23812014R00119